CS-5   GENERAL APTITUDE AND ABILITIES SERIES

*This is your
PASSBOOK for...*

Test Practice Book for 100 Civil Service Jobs

*Test Preparation Study Guide
Questions & Answers*

COPYRIGHT NOTICE

This book is SOLELY intended for, is sold ONLY to, and its use is RESTRICTED to individual, bona fide applicants or candidates who qualify by virtue of having seriously filed applications for appropriate license, certificate, professional and/or promotional advancement, higher school matriculation, scholarship, or other legitimate requirements of education and/or governmental authorities.

This book is NOT intended for use, class instruction, tutoring, training, duplication, copying, reprinting, excerption, or adaptation, etc., by:

1) Other publishers
2) Proprietors and/or Instructors of "Coaching" and/or Preparatory Courses
3) Personnel and/or Training Divisions of commercial, industrial, and governmental organizations
4) Schools, colleges, or universities and/or their departments and staffs, including teachers and other personnel
5) Testing Agencies or Bureaus
6) Study groups which seek by the purchase of a single volume to copy and/or duplicate and/or adapt this material for use by the group as a whole without having purchased individual volumes for each of the members of the group
7) Et al.

Such persons would be in violation of appropriate Federal and State statutes.

PROVISION OF LICENSING AGREEMENTS – Recognized educational, commercial, industrial, and governmental institutions and organizations, and others legitimately engaged in educational pursuits, including training, testing, and measurement activities, may address request for a licensing agreement to the copyright owners, who will determine whether, and under what conditions, including fees and charges, the materials in this book may be used them. In other words, a licensing facility exists for the legitimate use of the material in this book on other than an individual basis. However, it is asseverated and affirmed here that the material in this book CANNOT be used without the receipt of the express permission of such a licensing agreement from the Publishers. Inquiries re licensing should be addressed to the company, attention rights and permissions department.

All rights reserved, including the right of reproduction in whole or in part, in any form or by any means, electronic or mechanical, including photocopying, recording, or by any information storage and retrieval system, without permission in writing from the Publisher.

Copyright © 2025 by
National Learning Corporation

212 Michael Drive, Syosset, NY 11791
(516) 921-8888 • www.passbooks.com
E-mail: info@passbooks.com

PASSBOOK® SERIES

THE *PASSBOOK® SERIES* has been created to prepare applicants and candidates for the ultimate academic battlefield – the examination room.

At some time in our lives, each and every one of us may be required to take an examination – for validation, matriculation, admission, qualification, registration, certification, or licensure.

Based on the assumption that every applicant or candidate has met the basic formal educational standards, has taken the required number of courses, and read the necessary texts, the *PASSBOOK® SERIES* furnishes the one special preparation which may assure passing with confidence, instead of failing with insecurity. Examination questions – together with answers – are furnished as the basic vehicle for study so that the mysteries of the examination and its compounding difficulties may be eliminated or diminished by a sure method.

This book is meant to help you pass your examination provided that you qualify and are serious in your objective.

The entire field is reviewed through the huge store of content information which is succinctly presented through a provocative and challenging approach – the question-and-answer method.

A climate of success is established by furnishing the correct answers at the end of each test.

You soon learn to recognize types of questions, forms of questions, and patterns of questioning. You may even begin to anticipate expected outcomes.

You perceive that many questions are repeated or adapted so that you can gain acute insights, which may enable you to score many sure points.

You learn how to confront new questions, or types of questions, and to attack them confidently and work out the correct answers.

You note objectives and emphases, and recognize pitfalls and dangers, so that you may make positive educational adjustments.

Moreover, you are kept fully informed in relation to new concepts, methods, practices, and directions in the field.

You discover that you are actually taking the examination all the time: you are preparing for the examination by "taking" an examination, not by reading extraneous and/or supererogatory textbooks.

In short, this PASSBOOK®, used directedly, should be an important factor in helping you to pass your test.

TEST PRACTICE BOOK
FOR 100 CIVIL SERVICE JOBS

This book gives practice tests in common areas tested in many civil service exams, including:

- Verbal Abilities
- Clerical Abilities
- Reading Comprehension
- Arithmetic
- Preparing Written Material
- Report Writing
- Abstract Reasoning
- Number and Letter Series
- Interviewing

HOW TO TAKE A TEST

You have studied long, hard and conscientiously.

With your official admission card in hand, and your heart pounding, you have been admitted to the examination room.

You note that there are several hundred other applicants in the examination room waiting to take the same test.

They all appear to be equally well prepared.

You know that nothing but your best effort will suffice. The "moment of truth" is at hand: you now have to demonstrate objectively, in writing, your knowledge of content and your understanding of subject matter.

You are fighting the most important battle of your life—to pass and/or score high on an examination which will determine your career and provide the economic basis for your livelihood.

What extra, special things should you know and should you do in taking the examination?

I. YOU MUST PASS AN EXAMINATION

A. WHAT EVERY CANDIDATE SHOULD KNOW
Examination applicants often ask us for help in preparing for the written test. What can I study in advance? What kinds of questions will be asked? How will the test be given? How will the papers be graded?

B. HOW ARE EXAMS DEVELOPED?
Examinations are carefully written by trained technicians who are specialists in the field known as "psychological measurement," in consultation with recognized authorities in the field of work that the test will cover. These experts recommend the subject matter areas or skills to be tested; only those knowledges or skills important to your success on the job are included. The most reliable books and source materials available are used as references. Together, the experts and technicians judge the difficulty level of the questions.
Test technicians know how to phrase questions so that the problem is clearly stated. Their ethics do not permit "trick" or "catch" questions. Questions may have been tried out on sample groups, or subjected to statistical analysis, to determine their usefulness.
Written tests are often used in combination with performance tests, ratings of training and experience, and oral interviews. All of these measures combine to form the best-known means of finding the right person for the right job.

II. HOW TO PASS THE WRITTEN TEST

A. BASIC STEPS

1) Study the announcement

How, then, can you know what subjects to study? Our best answer is: "Learn as much as possible about the class of positions for which you've applied." The exam will test the knowledge, skills and abilities needed to do the work.

Your most valuable source of information about the position you want is the official exam announcement. This announcement lists the training and experience qualifications. Check these standards and apply only if you come reasonably close to meeting them. Many jurisdictions preview the written test in the exam announcement by including a section called "Knowledge and Abilities Required," "Scope of the Examination," or some similar heading. Here you will find out specifically what fields will be tested.

2) Choose appropriate study materials

If the position for which you are applying is technical or advanced, you will read more advanced, specialized material. If you are already familiar with the basic principles of your field, elementary textbooks would waste your time. Concentrate on advanced textbooks and technical periodicals. Think through the concepts and review difficult problems in your field.

These are all general sources. You can get more ideas on your own initiative, following these leads. For example, training manuals and publications of the government agency which employs workers in your field can be useful, particularly for technical and professional positions. A letter or visit to the government department involved may result in more specific study suggestions, and certainly will provide you with a more definite idea of the exact nature of the position you are seeking.

3) Study this book!

III. KINDS OF TESTS

Tests are used for purposes other than measuring knowledge and ability to perform specified duties. For some positions, it is equally important to test ability to make adjustments to new situations or to profit from training. In others, basic mental abilities not dependent on information are essential. Questions which test these things may not appear as pertinent to the duties of the position as those which test for knowledge and information. Yet they are often highly important parts of a fair examination. For very general questions, it is almost impossible to help you direct your study efforts. What we can do is to point out some of the more common of these general abilities needed in public service positions and describe some typical questions.

1) General information

Broad, general information has been found useful for predicting job success in some kinds of work. This is tested in a variety of ways, from vocabulary lists to questions about current events. Basic background in some field of work, such as sociology or economics, may be sampled in a group of questions. Often these are principles which have become familiar to most persons through exposure rather than through formal training. It is difficult to advise you how to study for these questions; being alert to the world around you is our best suggestion.

2) Verbal ability
An example of an ability needed in many positions is verbal or language ability. Verbal ability is, in brief, the ability to use and understand words. Vocabulary and grammar tests are typical measures of this ability. Reading comprehension or paragraph interpretation questions are common in many kinds of civil service tests. You are given a paragraph of written material and asked to find its central meaning.

IV. KINDS OF QUESTIONS

1. Multiple-choice Questions
Most popular of the short-answer questions is the "multiple choice" or "best answer" question. It can be used, for example, to test for factual knowledge, ability to solve problems or judgment in meeting situations found at work.
A multiple-choice question is normally one of three types:
- It can begin with an incomplete statement followed by several possible endings. You are to find the one ending which best completes the statement, although some of the others may not be entirely wrong.
- It can also be a complete statement in the form of a question which is answered by choosing one of the statements listed.
- It can be in the form of a problem – again you select the best answer.

Here is an example of a multiple-choice question with a discussion which should give you some clues as to the method for choosing the right answer:

When an employee has a complaint about his assignment, the action which will best help him overcome his difficulty is to
    A. discuss his difficulty with his coworkers
    B. take the problem to the head of the organization
    C. take the problem to the person who gave him the assignment
    D. say nothing to anyone about his complaint

In answering this question, you should study each of the choices to find which is best. Consider choice "A" – Certainly an employee may discuss his complaint with fellow employees, but no change or improvement can result, and the complaint remains unresolved. Choice "B" is a poor choice since the head of the organization probably does not know what assignment you have been given, and taking your problem to him is known as "going over the head" of the supervisor. The supervisor, or person who made the assignment, is the person who can clarify it or correct any injustice. Choice "C" is, therefore, correct. To say nothing, as in choice "D," is unwise. Supervisors have and interest in knowing the problems employees are facing, and the employee is seeking a solution to his problem.

2. True/False

3. Matching Questions
Matching an answer from a column of choices within another column.

V. RECORDING YOUR ANSWERS

Computer terminals are used more and more today for many different kinds of exams.

For an examination with very few applicants, you may be told to record your answers in the test booklet itself. Separate answer sheets are much more common. If this separate answer sheet is to be scored by machine – and this is often the case – it is highly important that you mark your answers correctly in order to get credit.

VI. BEFORE THE TEST

YOUR PHYSICAL CONDITION IS IMPORTANT

If you are not well, you can't do your best work on tests. If you are half asleep, you can't do your best either. Here are some tips:

1) Get about the same amount of sleep you usually get. Don't stay up all night before the test, either partying or worrying—DON'T DO IT!
2) If you wear glasses, be sure to wear them when you go to take the test. This goes for hearing aids, too.
3) If you have any physical problems that may keep you from doing your best, be sure to tell the person giving the test. If you are sick or in poor health, you relay cannot do your best on any test. You can always come back and take the test some other time.

Common sense will help you find procedures to follow to get ready for an examination. Too many of us, however, overlook these sensible measures. Indeed, nervousness and fatigue have been found to be the most serious reasons why applicants fail to do their best on civil service tests. Here is a list of reminders:

- Begin your preparation early – Don't wait until the last minute to go scurrying around for books and materials or to find out what the position is all about.
- Prepare continuously – An hour a night for a week is better than an all-night cram session. This has been definitely established. What is more, a night a week for a month will return better dividends than crowding your study into a shorter period of time.
- Locate the place of the exam – You have been sent a notice telling you when and where to report for the examination. If the location is in a different town or otherwise unfamiliar to you, it would be well to inquire the best route and learn something about the building.
- Relax the night before the test – Allow your mind to rest. Do not study at all that night. Plan some mild recreation or diversion; then go to bed early and get a good night's sleep.
- Get up early enough to make a leisurely trip to the place for the test – This way unforeseen events, traffic snarls, unfamiliar buildings, etc. will not upset you.
- Dress comfortably – A written test is not a fashion show. You will be known by number and not by name, so wear something comfortable.
- Leave excess paraphernalia at home – Shopping bags and odd bundles will get in your way. You need bring only the items mentioned in the official notice you received; usually everything you need is provided. Do not bring reference books to the exam. They will only confuse those last minutes and be taken away from you when in the test room.

- Arrive somewhat ahead of time – If because of transportation schedules you must get there very early, bring a newspaper or magazine to take your mind off yourself while waiting.
- Locate the examination room – When you have found the proper room, you will be directed to the seat or part of the room where you will sit. Sometimes you are given a sheet of instructions to read while you are waiting. Do not fill out any forms until you are told to do so; just read them and be prepared.
- Relax and prepare to listen to the instructions
- If you have any physical problem that may keep you from doing your best, be sure to tell the test administrator. If you are sick or in poor health, you really cannot do your best on the exam. You can come back and take the test some other time.

VII. AT THE TEST

The day of the test is here and you have the test booklet in your hand. The temptation to get going is very strong. Caution! There is more to success than knowing the right answers. You must know how to identify your papers and understand variations in the type of short-answer question used in this particular examination. Follow these suggestions for maximum results from your efforts:

1) Cooperate with the monitor

The test administrator has a duty to create a situation in which you can be as much at ease as possible. He will give instructions, tell you when to begin, check to see that you are marking your answer sheet correctly, and so on. He is not there to guard you, although he will see that your competitors do not take unfair advantage. He wants to help you do your best.

2) Listen to all instructions

Don't jump the gun! Wait until you understand all directions. In most civil service tests you get more time than you need to answer the questions. So don't be in a hurry. Read each word of instructions until you clearly understand the meaning. Study the examples, listen to all announcements and follow directions. Ask questions if you do not understand what to do.

3) Identify your papers

Civil service exams are usually identified by number only. You will be assigned a number; you must not put your name on your test papers. Be sure to copy your number correctly. Since more than one exam may be given, copy your exact examination title.

4) Plan your time

Unless you are told that a test is a "speed" or "rate of work" test, speed itself is usually not important. Time enough to answer all the questions will be provided, but this does not mean that you have all day. An overall time limit has been set. Divide the total time (in minutes) by the number of questions to determine the approximate time you have for each question.

5) Do not linger over difficult questions

If you come across a difficult question, mark it with a paper clip (useful to have along) and come back to it when you have been through the booklet. One caution if you do this – be sure to skip a number on your answer sheet as well. Check often to be sure that you have not lost your place and that you are marking in the row numbered the same as the question you are answering.

6) Read the questions

Be sure you know what the question asks! Many capable people are unsuccessful because they failed to read the questions correctly.

7) Answer all questions

Unless you have been instructed that a penalty will be deducted for incorrect answers, it is better to guess than to omit a question.

8) Speed tests

It is often better NOT to guess on speed tests. It has been found that on timed tests people are tempted to spend the last few seconds before time is called in marking answers at random – without even reading them – in the hope of picking up a few extra points. To discourage this practice, the instructions may warn you that your score will be "corrected" for guessing. That is, a penalty will be applied. The incorrect answers will be deducted from the correct ones, or some other penalty formula will be used.

9) Review your answers

If you finish before time is called, go back to the questions you guessed or omitted to give them further thought. Review other answers if you have time.

10) Return your test materials

If you are ready to leave before others have finished or time is called, take ALL your materials to the monitor and leave quietly. Never take any test material with you. The monitor can discover whose papers are not complete, and taking a test booklet may be grounds for disqualification.

VIII. EXAMINATION TECHNIQUES

1) Read the general instructions carefully. These are usually printed on the first page of the exam booklet. As a rule, these instructions refer to the timing of the examination; the fact that you should not start work until the signal and must stop work at a signal, etc. If there are any special instructions, such as a choice of questions to be answered, make sure that you note this instruction carefully.

2) When you are ready to start work on the examination, that is as soon as the signal has been given, read the instructions to each question booklet, underline any key words or phrases, such as least, best, outline, describe and the like. In this way you will tend to answer as requested rather than discover on reviewing your paper that you listed without describing, that you selected the worst choice rather than the best choice, etc.

3) If the examination is of the objective or multiple-choice type – that is, each question will also give a series of possible answers: A, B, C or D, and you are called upon to select the best answer and write the letter next to that answer on your answer paper – it is advisable to start answering each question in turn. There may be anywhere from 50 to 100 such questions in the three or four hours allotted and you can see how much time would be taken if you read through all the questions before beginning to answer any. Furthermore, if you

come across a question or group of questions which you know would be difficult to answer, it would undoubtedly affect your handling of all the other questions.

4) If the examination is of the essay type and contains but a few questions, it is a moot point as to whether you should read all the questions before starting to answer any one. Of course, if you are given a choice – say five out of seven and the like – then it is essential to read all the questions so you can eliminate the two that are most difficult. If, however, you are asked to answer all the questions, there may be danger in trying to answer the easiest one first because you may find that you will spend too much time on it. The best technique is to answer the first question, then proceed to the second, etc.

5) Time your answers. Before the exam begins, write down the time it started, then add the time allowed for the examination and write down the time it must be completed, then divide the time available somewhat as follows:
    - If 3-1/2 hours are allowed, that would be 210 minutes. If you have 80 objective-type questions, that would be an average of 2-1/2 minutes per question. Allow yourself no more than 2 minutes per question, or a total of 160 minutes, which will permit about 50 minutes to review.
    - If for the time allotment of 210 minutes there are 7 essay questions to answer, that would average about 30 minutes a question. Give yourself only 25 minutes per question so that you have about 35 minutes to review.

6) The most important instruction is to read each question and make sure you know what is wanted. The second most important instruction is to time yourself properly so that you answer every question. The third most important instruction is to answer every question. Guess if you have to but include something for each question. Remember that you will receive no credit for a blank and will probably receive some credit if you write something in answer to an essay question. If you guess a letter – say "B" for a multiple-choice question – you may have guessed right. If you leave a blank as an answer to a multiple-choice question, the examiners may respect your feelings but it will not add a point to your score. Some exams may penalize you for wrong answers, so in such cases only, you may not want to guess unless you have some basis for your answer.

7) Suggestions
    a. Objective-type questions
        1. Examine the question booklet for proper sequence of pages and questions
        2. Read all instructions carefully
        3. Skip any question which seems too difficult; return to it after all other questions have been answered
        4. Apportion your time properly; do not spend too much time on any single question or group of questions
        5. Note and underline key words – all, most, fewest, least, best, worst, same, opposite, etc.
        6. Pay particular attention to negatives
        7. Note unusual option, e.g., unduly long, short, complex, different or similar in content to the body of the question
        8. Observe the use of "hedging" words – probably, may, most likely, etc.

9. Make sure that your answer is put next to the same number as the question
10. Do not second-guess unless you have good reason to believe the second answer is definitely more correct
11. Cross out original answer if you decide another answer is more accurate; do not erase until you are ready to hand your paper in
12. Answer all questions; guess unless instructed otherwise
13. Leave time for review

b. Essay questions
1. Read each question carefully
2. Determine exactly what is wanted. Underline key words or phrases.
3. Decide on outline or paragraph answer
4. Include many different points and elements unless asked to develop any one or two points or elements
5. Show impartiality by giving pros and cons unless directed to select one side only
6. Make and write down any assumptions you find necessary to answer the questions
7. Watch your English, grammar, punctuation and choice of words
8. Time your answers; don't crowd material

8) Answering the essay question

Most essay questions can be answered by framing the specific response around several key words or ideas. Here are a few such key words or ideas:

M's: manpower, materials, methods, money, management
P's: purpose, program, policy, plan, procedure, practice, problems, pitfalls, personnel, public relations

a. Six basic steps in handling problems:
1. Preliminary plan and background development
2. Collect information, data and facts
3. Analyze and interpret information, data and facts
4. Analyze and develop solutions as well as make recommendations
5. Prepare report and sell recommendations
6. Install recommendations and follow up effectiveness

b. Pitfalls to avoid
1. Taking things for granted – A statement of the situation does not necessarily imply that each of the elements is necessarily true; for example, a complaint may be invalid and biased so that all that can be taken for granted is that a complaint has been registered
2. Considering only one side of a situation – Wherever possible, indicate several alternatives and then point out the reasons you selected the best one
3. Failing to indicate follow up – Whenever your answer indicates action on your part, make certain that you will take proper follow-up action to see how successful your recommendations, procedures or actions turn out to be
4. Taking too long in answering any single question – Remember to time your answers properly

EXAMINATION SECTION

VERBAL ABILITIES TEST
DIRECTIONS AND SAMPLE QUESTIONS

Study the sample questions carefully. Each question has four suggested answers. Decide which one is the best answer. Find the question number on the Sample Answer Sheet. Show your answer to the question by printing the letter of the correct answer in the space at the right. If you have to erase a mark, be sure to erase it completely. Mark only one answer for each question. Do NOT mark space E for any question.

SAMPLE VERBAL QUESTIONS

I. *Previous* means MOST NEARLY I.____
   A. abandoned   B. former   C. timely   D. younger

II. (Reading) "Just as the procedure of a collection department must be clear cut II.____
    and definite, the steps being taken with the sureness of a skilled chess player, so the various paragraphs of a collection letter must show clear organization, giving evidence of a mind that, from the beginning, has had a specific end in view."
    The quotation BEST supports the statement that a collection letter should always
    A. show a spirit of sportsmanship   B. be divided into several paragraphs
    C. be brief, but courteous   D. be carefully planned

III. Decide which sentence is preferable with respect to grammar and usage suitable III.____
     for a formal letter or report.
     A. They do not ordinarily present these kind of reports in detail like this.
     B. A report of this kind is not hardly ever given in such detail as this one.
     C. This report is more detailed than what such reports ordinarily are.
     D. A report of this kind is not ordinarily presented in as much detail as this one is.

IV. Find the correct spelling of the word and print the letter of the correct answer in IV.____
    the space at the right. If no suggested spelling is correct, print the letter D.
    A. athalete   B. athelete   C. athlete   D. none of these

V. SPEEDOMETER is related to POINTER as WATCH is related to V.____
   A. case   B. hands   C. dial   D. numerals

1

EXAMINATION SECTION

TEST 1

DIRECTIONS: Each question or incomplete statement is followed by several suggested answers or completions. Select the one that BEST answers the question or completes the statement. *PRINT THE LETTER OF THE CORRECT ANSWER IN THE SPACE AT THE RIGHT.*

1. *Flexible* means MOST NEARLY
   A. breakable   B. flammable   C. pliable   D. weak

2. *Option* means MOST NEARLY
   A. use   B. choice   C. value   D. blame

3. To *verify* means MOST NEARLY to
   A. examine   B. explain   C. confirm   D. guarantee

4. *Indolent* means MOST NEARLY
   A. moderate   B. happiness   C. selfish   D. lazy

5. *Respiration* means MOST NEARLY
   A. recovery   B. breathing   C. pulsation   D. sweating

6. PLUMBER is related to WRENCH as PAINTER related to
   A. brush   B. pipe   C. shop   D. hammer

7. LETTER is related to MESSAGE as PACKAGE is related to
   A. sender   B. merchandise
   C. insurance   D. business

8. FOOD is related to HUNGER as SLEEP is related to
   A. night   B. dream   C. weariness   D. rest

9. KEY is related to TYPEWRITER as DIAL is related to
   A. sun   B. number   C. circle   D. telephone

GRAMMAR

10. A. I think that they will promote whoever has the best record.
    B. The firm would have liked to have promoted all employees with good records.
    C. Such of them that have the best records have excellent prospects of promotion.
    D. I feel sure they will give the promotion to whomever has the best record.

11.   A. The receptionist must answer courteously the questions of all them callers.
      B. The receptionist must answer courteously the questions what are asked by the callers.
      C. There would have been no trouble if the receptionist had have always answered courteously.
      D. The receptionist should answer courteously the questions of all callers.

11.____

SPELLING

12.   A. collapsible   B. colapseble
      C. collapseble   D. none of the above

12.____

13.   A. ambigeuous   B. ambigeous
      C. ambiguous   D. none of the above

13.____

14.   A. predesessor   B. predecesar
      C. predecesser   D. none of the above

14.____

15.   A. sanctioned   B. sancktioned
      C. sanctionned   D. none of the above

15.____

READING

16.   "The secretarial profession is a very old one and has increased in importance with the passage of time. In modern times, the vast expansion of business and industry has greatly increased the need and opportunities for secretaries, and for the first time in history their number has become large."
      The above quotation BEST supports the statement that the secretarial profession
         A. is older than business and industry
         B. did not exist in ancient times
         C. has greatly increased in size
         D. demands higher training than it did formerly

16.____

17.   "Civilization started to move ahead more rapidly when man freed himself of the shackles that restricted his search for the truth."
      The above quotation BEST supports the statement that the progress of civilization
         A. came as a result of man's dislike for obstacles
         B. did not begin until restrictions on learning were removed
         C. has been aided by man's efforts to find
         D. the truth is based on continually increasing efforts

17.____

18.   *Vigilant* means MOST NEARLY
         A. sensible   B. watchful   C. suspicious   D. restless

18.____

19.   *Incidental* means MOST NEARLY
         A. independent   B. needless   C. infrequent   D. casual

19.____

20. *Conciliatory* means MOST NEARLY
    A. pacific   B. contentious   C. obligatory   D. offensive

21. *Altercation* means MOST NEARLY
    A. defeat
    B. concurrence
    C. controversy
    D. vexation

22. *Irresolute* means MOST NEARLY
    A. wavering
    B. insubordinate
    C. impudent
    D. unobservant

23. DARKNESS is related to SUNLIGHT as STILLNESS is related to
    A. quiet   B. moonlight   C. sound   D. dark

24. DESIGNED is related to INTENTION as ACCIDENTAL is related to
    A. purpose   B. caution   C. damage   D. chance

25. ERROR is related to PRACTICE as SOUND is related to
    A. deafness   B. noise   C. muffler   D. horn

26. RESEARCH is related to FINDINGS as TRAINING is related to
    A. skill
    B. tests
    C. supervision
    D. teaching

27. A. If properly addressed, the letter will reach my mother and I.
    B. The letter had been addressed to myself and my mother.
    C. I believe the letter was addressed to either my mother or I.
    D. My mother's name, as well as mine, was on the letter.

28. A. The supervisor reprimanded the typist, whom she believed had made careless errors.
    B. The typist would have corrected the errors had she of known that the supervisor would see the report.
    C. The errors in the typed report were so numerous that they could hardly be overlooked.
    D. Many errors were found in the report which she typed and could not disregard them.

29. A. miniature   B. minneature
    C. mineature   D. none of the above

30. A. extemporaneous   B. extempuraneus
    C. extemporaneous   D. none of the above

31. A. problemmatical   B. problematical
    C. problematicle   D. none of the above

32. A. descendant   B. decendant
    C. desendant   D. none of the above

33. "The likelihood of America's exhausting her natural resources seems to be growing less. All kinds of waste are being reworked and new uses are constantly being found for almost everything. We are getting more use out of our goods and are making many new byproducts out of what was formerly thrown away."
The above quotation BEST supports the statement that we seem to be in less danger of exhausting our resources because
A. economy is found to lie in the use of substitutes
B. more service is obtained from a given amount of material
C. we are allowing time for nature to restore them
D. supply and demand are better controlled

34. "Memos should be clear, concise, and brief. Omit all unnecessary words. The parts of speech most often used in memos are nouns, verbs, adjectives, and adverbs. If possible, do without pronouns, prepositions, articles, and copulative verbs. Use simple sentences, rather than complex or compound ones.
The above quotation BEST supports the statement that in writing memos one should always use
A. common and simple words
B. only nouns, verbs, adjectives, and adverbs
C. incomplete sentences
D. only the word essential to the meaning

35. To *counteract* means MOST NEARLY to
A. undermine   B. censure   C. preserve   D. neutralize

36. *Deferred* means MOST NEARLY
A. reversed   B. delayed
C. considered   D. forbidden

37. *Feasible* means MOST NEARLY
A. capable   B. justifiable   C. practicable   D. beneficial

38. To *encounter* means MOST NEARLY to
A. meet   B. recall   C. overcome   D. retreat

39. *Innate* means MOST NEARLY
A. eternal   B. well-developed
C. native   D. prospective

40. STUDENT is to TEACHER as DISCIPLE is related to
A. follower   B. master   C. principal   D. pupil

41. LECTURE is related to AUDITORIUM as EXPERIMENT is related to
A. scientist   B. chemistry   C. laboratory   D. discovery

42. BODY is related to FOOD as ENGINE is related to
A. wheels   B. fuel   C. motion   D. smoke

43. SCHOOL is related to EDUCATION as THEATER is related to   43._____
    A. management   B. stage
    C. recreation   D. preparation

44. A. Most all these statements have been supported by persons who are   44._____
       reliable and can be depended upon.
    B. The persons which have guaranteed these statements are reliable.
    C. Reliable persons guarantee the facts with regards to the truth of these
       statements.
    D. These statements can be depended on, for their truth has been guaranteed
       by reliable persons.

45. A. The success of the book pleased both his publisher and he.   45._____
    B. Both his publisher and he was pleased with the success of the book.
    C. Neither he or his publisher was disappointed with the success of the book.
    D. His publisher was as pleased as he with the success of the book.

46. A. extercate   B. extracate   46._____
    C. extricate   D. none of the above

47. A. hereditory   B. hereditary   47._____
    C. hereditairy   D. none of the above

48. A. auspiceous   B. auspiseous   48._____
    C. auspicious   D. none of the above

49. A. sequance   B. sequence   49._____
    C. sequense   D. none of the above

50. "The prevention of accidents makes it necessary not only that safety devices   50._____
    be used to guard exposed machinery but also that mechanics be instructed in
    safety rules which they must follow for their own protection, and that the lighting
    in the plant be adequate."
    The above quotation BEST supports the statement that industrial accidents
    A. may be due to ignorance
    B. are always avoidable
    C. usually result from inadequate machinery
    D. cannot be entirely overcome

51. "The English language is peculiarly rich in synonyms, and there is scarcely a   51._____
    language spoken among men that has not some representative in English
    speech. The spirit of the Anglo-Saxon race has subjugate these various
    elements to one idiom, making not a patchwork, but a composite language."
    The above quotation BEST supports the statement that the English language
    A. has few idiomatic expressions
    B. is difficult to translate
    C. is used universally
    D. has absorbed words from other languages

52. To *acquiesce* means MOST NEARLY to
    A. assent   B. acquire   C. complete   D. participate

53. *Unanimity* means MOST NEARLY
    A. emphasis
    B. namelessness
    C. harmony
    D. impartiality

54. *Precedent* means MOST NEARLY
    A. example   B. theory   C. law   D. conformity

55. *Versatile* means MOST NEARLY
    A. broad-minded
    B. well-known
    C. up-to-date
    D. many-sided

56. *Authentic* means MOST NEARLY
    A. detailed   B. reliable   C. valuable   D. practical

57. BIOGRAPHY is related to FACT as NOVEL is related to
    A. fiction   B. literature   C. narration   D. book

58. COPY is related to CARBON PAPER as MOTION PICTURE is related to
    A. theater   B. film   C. duplicate   D. television

59. EFFICIENCY is related to REWARD as CARELESSNESS is related to
    A. improvement
    B. disobedience
    C. reprimand
    D. repetition

60. ABUNDANT is related to CHEAP as SCARCE is related to
    A. ample
    B. costly
    C. inexpensive
    D. unobtainable

61. A. Brown's & Company employees have recently received increases in salary.
    B. Brown & Company recently increased the salaries of all its employees.
    C. Recently, Brown & Company has increased their employees' salaries.
    D. Brown & Company have recently increased the salaries of all its employees.

62. A. In reviewing the typists' work reports, the job analyst found records of unusual typing speeds.
    B. It says in the job analyst's report that some employees type with great speed.
    C. The job analyst found that, in reviewing the typists' work reports, that some unusual typing speeds had been made.
    D. In the reports of typists' speeds, the job analyst found some records that are kind of unusual.

63. A. obliterate
    B. oblitterat
    C. obliterate
    D. none of the above

64. A. diagnosis B. diagnosis
    C. diagnosis D. none of the above
    64.____

65. A. contenance B. countenance
    C. knowledge D. none of the above
    65.____

66. A. conceivably B. concieveably
    C. conceiveably D. none of the above
    66.____

67. "Through advertising, manufacturers exercise a high degree of control over consumers' desires. However, the manufacturer assumes enormous risks in attempting to predict what consumers will want and in producing goods in quantity and distributing them in advance of final selection by the consumers." The above quotation BEST supports the statement that manufacturers
    A. can eliminate the risk of overproduction by advertising
    B. distribute goods directly to the consumers
    C. must depend upon the final consumers for the success of their undertakings
    D. can predict with great accuracy the success of any product they put on the market
    67.____

68. "In the relations of man to nature, the procuring of food and shelter is fundamental. With the migration of man to various climates, ever new adjustments to the food supply and to the climate became necessary." The above quotation BEST supports the statement that the means by which man supplies his material needs are
    A. accidental B. varied C. limited D. inadequate
    68.____

69. *Strident* means MOST NEARLY
    A. swaggering B. domineering
    C. angry D. harsh
    69.____

70. To *confine* means MOST NEARLY to
    A. hide B. restrict C. eliminate D. punish
    70.____

71. To *accentuate* means MOST NEARLY to
    A. modify B. hasten C. sustain D. intensify
    71.____

72. *Banal* means MOST NEARLY
    A. commonplace B. forceful
    C. tranquil D. indifferent
    72.____

73. *Incorrigible* means MOST NEARLY
    A. intolerable B. retarded
    C. irreformable D. brazen
    73.____

74. POLICEMAN is related to ORDER as DOCTOR is related to
    A. physician B. hospital C. sickness D. health
    74.____

75. ARTIST is related to EASEL as WEAVER is related to
    A. loom   B. cloth   C. threads   D. spinner

76. CROWD is related to PERSONS as FLEET is related to
    A. expedition   B. officers   C. navy   D. ships

77. CALENDAR is related to DATE as MAP is related to
    A. geography   B. trip   C. mileage   D. vacation

78. A. Since the report lacked the needed information, it was of no use to him.
    B. This report was useless to him because there were no needed information in it.
    C. Since the report did not contain the needed information, it was not real useful to him.
    D. Being that the report lacked the needed information, he could not use it.

79. A. The company had hardly declared the dividend till the notices were prepared for mailing.
    B. They had no sooner declared the dividend when they sent the notices to the stockholders.
    C. No sooner had the dividend been declared than the notices were prepared for mailing.
    D. Scarcely had the dividend been declared than the notices were sent out.

80. A. compitition   B. competition
    C. competetion   D. none of the above

81. A. occassion   B. ocassion
    C. occasion   D. none of the above

82. A. knowlege   B. knowledge
    C. knolledge D. none of the above

83. A. deliborate   B. deliberate
    C. deliberate   D. none of the above

84. "What constitutes skill in any line of work is not always easy to determine; economy of time must be carefully distinguished from economy of energy, as the quickest method may require the greatest expenditure of muscular effort, and may not be essential or at all desirable."
    The above quotation BEST supports the statement that
    A. the most efficiently executed task is not always the one done in the shortest time
    B. energy and time cannot both be conserved in performing a single task
    C. a task is well done when it is performed in the shortest time
    D. skill in performing a task should not be acquired at the expense of time

85. "It is difficult to distinguish between bookkeeping and accounting. In attempts to do so, bookkeeping is called the art, and accounting the science, of recording business transactions. Bookkeeping gives the history of the business in a systematic manner; and accounting classifies, analyzes, and interpret the facts thus recorded."

The above quotation BEST supports the statement that
- A. accounting is less systematic than bookkeeping
- B. accounting and bookkeeping are closely related
- C. bookkeeping and accounting cannot be distinguished from one another
- D. bookkeeping has been superseded by accounting

85.____

KEY (CORRECT ANSWERS)

1.	C	16.	C	31.	B	46.	C	61.	B	76. D
2.	B	17.	C	32.	A	47.	B	62.	A	77. C
3.	C	18.	B	33.	B	48.	C	63.	A	78. A
4.	D	19.	D	34.	D	49.	B	64.	C	79. C
5.	B	20.	A	35.	D	50.	A	65.	B	80. B
6.	A	21.	C	36.	B	51.	D	66.	A	81. B
7.	B	22.	A	37.	C	52.	A	67.	C	82. C
8.	C	23.	C	38.	A	53.	C	68.	B	83. B
9.	D	24.	D	39.	C	54.	A	69.	D	84. A
10.	A	25.	C	40.	B	55.	D	70.	B	85. B
11.	D	26.	A	41.	C	56.	B	71.	D	
12.	A	27.	D	42.	B	57.	A	72.	A	
13.	C	28.	C	43.	C	58.	B	73.	C	
14.	D	29.	D	44.	D	59.	C	74.	D	
15.	A	30.	A	45.	D	60.	B	75.	A	

TEST 2

DIRECTIONS: Each question or incomplete statement is followed by several suggested answers or completions. Select the one that BEST answers the question or completes the statement. *PRINT THE LETTER OF THE CORRECT ANSWER IN THE SPACE AT THE RIGHT.*

1. *Option* means MOST NEARLY
   - A. use
   - B. choice
   - C. value
   - D. blame
   - E. mistake

   1._____

2. *Irresolute* means MOST NEARLY
   - A. wavering
   - B. insubordinate
   - C. impudent
   - D. determined
   - E. unobservant

   2._____

3. *Flexible* means MOST NEARLY
   - A. breakable
   - B. inflammable
   - C. pliable
   - D. weak
   - E. impervious

   3._____

4. To *counteract* means MOST NEARLY to
   - A. undermine
   - B. censure
   - C. preserve
   - D. sustain
   - E. neutralize

   4._____

5. To *verify* means MOST NEARLY to
   - A. justify
   - B. explain
   - C. confirm
   - D. guarantee
   - E. examine

   5._____

6. *Indolent* means MOST NEARLY
   - A. moderate
   - B. relentless
   - C. selfish
   - D. lazy
   - E. hopeless

   6._____

7. To say that an action is *deferred* means MOST NEARLY that it is
   - A. delayed
   - B. reversed
   - C. considered
   - D. forbidden
   - E. followed

   7._____

8. To *encounter* means MOST NEARLY to
   - A. meet
   - B. recall
   - C. overcome
   - D. weaken
   - E. retreat

   8._____

9. *Feasible* means MOST NEARLY
   - A. capable
   - B. practicable
   - C. justifiable
   - D. beneficial
   - E. reliable

   9._____

10. *Respiration* means MOST NEARLY
    - A. dehydration
    - B. breathing
    - C. pulsation
    - D. sweating
    - E. recovery

    10._____

11. *Vigilant* means MOST NEARLY
    A. sensible   B. ambitious   C. watchful
    D. suspicious E. restless

12. To say that an action is taken *before the proper time* means MOST NEARLY that it is taken
    A. prematurely B. furtively   C. temporarily
    D. punctually   E. presently

13. *Innate* means MOST NEARLY
    A. eternal   B. learned   C. native
    D. prospective E. well-developed

14. *Precedent* means MOST NEARLY
    A. duplicate   B. theory   C. law
    D. conformity   E. example

15. To say that the flow of work into an office is *incessant* means MOST NEARLY that it is
    A. more than can be handled   B. uninterrupted
    C. scanty   D. decreasing in volume
    E. orderly

16. *Unanimity* means MOST NEARLY
    A. emphasis   B. namelessness   C. disagreement
    D. harmony   E. impartiality

17. *Incidental* means MOST NEARLY
    A. independent   B. needless   C. infrequent
    D. necessary   E. casual

18. *Versatile* means MOST NEARLY
    A. broad-minded B. well-known   C. old-fashioned
    D. many-sided   E. up-to-date

19. *Conciliatory* means MOST NEARLY
    A. pacific   B. contentious   C. disorderly
    D. obligatory E. offensive

20. *Altercation* means MOST NEARLY
    A. defeat   B. concurrence   C. controversy
    D. consensus   E. vexation

21. "The secretarial profession is a very old one and has increased in importance with the passage of time. In modern times, the vast expansion of business and industry has greatly increased the need and opportunities for secretaries, and for the first time in history their number as become large."

The above quotation BEST supports the statement that the secretarial profession
- A. is older than business and industry
- B. did not exist in ancient times
- C. has greatly increased in size
- D. demands higher training than it did formerly
- E. has always had many members

22. "The modern system of production unites various kinds of workers into a well-organized body in which each has a definite place."
The above quotation BEST supports the statement that the modern system of production
- A. increases production
- B. trains workers
- C. simplifies tasks
- D. combines and places workers
- E. combines the various plants

22.____

23. "The prevention of accidents makes it necessary not only that safety devices be used to guard exposed machinery but also that mechanics be instructed in safety rules which they must follow for their own protection, and that the lighting in the plant be adequate.
The above quotation BEST supports the statement that industrial accidents
- A. may be due to ignorance
- B. are always avoidable
- C. usually result from inadequate machinery
- D. cannot be entirely overcome
- E. result in damage to machinery

23.____

24. "It is wise to choose a duplicating machine that will do the work required with the greatest efficiency and at the least cost. Users with a large volume of business need speedy machines that cost little to operate and are well made."
The above quotation BEST supports the statement that
- A. most users of duplicating machines prefer low operating cost to efficiency
- B. a well-built machine will outlast a cheap one
- C. a duplicating machine is not efficient unless it is sturdy
- D. a duplicating machine should be both efficient and economical
- E. in duplicating machines speed is more usual than low operating cost

24.____

25. "The likelihood of America's exhausting her natural resources seems to be growing less. All kinds of waste are being reworked and new uses are constantly being found for almost everything. We are getting more use out of our goods and are making many new byproducts out of what was formerly thrown away."
The above quotation BEST supports the statement that we seem to be in less danger of exhausting our resources because
- A. economy is found to lie in the use of substitutes
- B. more service is obtained from a given amount of material
- C. more raw materials are being produced
- D. supply and demand are better controlled
- E. we are allowing time for nature to restore them

25.____

4 (#2)

26. "Probably few people realize, as they drive on a concrete road, that steel is used to keep the surface flat and even, in spite of the weight of busses and trucks. Steel bars, deeply imbedded in the concrete, provide sinews to take the stresses so that they cannot crack the slab or make it wavy."
The above quotation BEST supports the statement that a concrete road
   A. is expensive to build
   B. usually cracks under heavy weights
   C. looks like any other road
   D. is used exclusively for heavy traffic
   E. is reinforced with other material

26.____

27. "Through advertising, manufacturers exercise a high degree of control over consumers' desires. However, the manufacturer assumes enormous risks in attempting to predict what consumers will want and in producing goods in quantity and distributing them in advance of final selection by the consumers."
The above quotation BEST supports the statement that manufacturers
   A. can eliminate the risk of overproduction by advertising
   B. completely control buyers' needs and desires
   C. must depend upon the final consumers for the success of their undertakings
   D. distribute goods directly to the consumers
   E. can predict with great accuracy the success of any product they put on the market

27.____

28. "Success in shorthand, like success in any other study, depends upon the interest the student takes in it. In writing shorthand, it is not sufficient to know how to write a word correctly; one must also be able to write it quickly."
The above quotation BEST supports the statement that
   A. one must be able to read shorthand as well as to write it
   B. shorthand requires much study
   C. if a student can write correctly, he can also write quickly
   D. proficiency in shorthand requires both speed and accuracy
   E. interest in shorthand makes study unnecessary

28.____

29. "The countries in the Western Hemisphere were settled by people who were ready each day for new adventure. The peoples of North and South America have retained, in addition to expectant and forward-looking attitudes, the ability and the willingness that they have often shown in the past to adapt themselves to new conditions.
The above quotation BEST supports the statement that the peoples in the Western Hemisphere
   A. no longer have fresh adventures daily
   B. are capable of making changes as new situations arise
   C. are no more forward-looking than the peoples of other regions
   D. tend to resist regulations
   E. differ considerably among themselves

29.____

30. "Civilization started to move ahead more rapidly when man freed himself of the shackles that restricted his search for the truth."
The above quotation BEST supports the statement that the progress of civilization
   A. came as a result of man's dislike for obstacles
   B. did not begin until restrictions on learning were removed
   C. has been aided by man's efforts to find the truth
   D. is based on continually increasing efforts
   E. continues at a constantly increasing rate

31. "It is difficult to distinguish between bookkeeping and accounting. In attempts to do so, bookkeeping is called the art, and accounting the science, of recording business transactions. Bookkeeping gives the history of the business in a systematic manner, and accounting classifies, analyzes, and interprets the facts thus recorded."
The above quotation BEST supports the statement that
   A. accounting is less systematic than bookkeeping
   B. accounting and bookkeeping are closely related
   C. bookkeeping and accounting cannot be distinguish from one another
   D. bookkeeping has been superseded by accounting
   E. the facts recorded by bookkeeping may be interpreted in many ways

32. "Some specialists are willing to give their services to the Government entirely free of charge; some feel that a nominal salary, such as will cover traveling expenses, is sufficient for a position that is recognized as being somewhat honorary in nature; many other specialists value their time so highly that they will not devote any of it to public service that does not repay them at a rate commensurate with the fees that they can obtain from a good private clientele."
The above quotation BEST supports the statement that the use of specialists by the Government
   A. is rare because of the high cost of securing such persons
   B. may be influenced by the willingness of specialists to serve
   C. enables them to secure higher salaries in private fields
   D. has become increasingly common during the past few years
   E. always conflicts with private demands for their services

33. "The leader of an industrial enterprise has two principal functions. He must manufacture and distribute a product at a profit, and he must keep individuals and groups of individuals working effectively together."
The above quotation BEST supports the statement that an industrial leader should be able to
   A. increase the distribution of his plant's product
   B. introduce large-scale production methods
   C. coordinate the activities of his employees
   D. profit by the experience of other leaders
   E. expand the business rapidly

34. "The coloration of textile fabrics composed of cotton and wool generally requires two processes, as the process used in dyeing wool is seldom capable of fixing the color upon cotton. The usual method is to immerse the fabric in the requisite baths to dye the wool and then to treat the partially dyed material in the manner found suitable for cotton."
The above quotation BEST supports the statement that the dyeing of textile fabrics composed of cotton and wool
    A. is less complicated than the dyeing of wool alone
    B. is more successful when the material contains more cotton than wool
    C. is not satisfactory when solid colors are desired
    D. is restricted to two colors for any one fabric
    E. is usually based upon the methods required for dyeing the different materials

35. "The fact must not be overlooked that only about one-half of the international trade of the world crosses the oceans. The other half is merely exchanges of merchandise between countries lying alongside each other or at least within the same continent."
The above quotation BEST supports the statement that
    A. the most important part of any country's trade is transoceanic
    B. domestic trade is insignificant when compared with foreign trade
    C. the exchange of goods between neighboring countries is not considered international trade
    D. foreign commerce is not necessarily carried on by water
    E. about one-half of the trade of the world is international

36. "In the relations of man to nature, the procuring of food and shelter is fundamental. With the migration of man to various climate, ever new adjustments to the food supply and to the climate became necessary."
The above quotation BEST supports the statement that the means by which man supplies his material needs are
    A. accidental   B. varied   C. limited
    D. uniform   E. inadequate

37. "Every language has its peculiar word associations that have no basis in logic and cannot therefore be reasoned about. These idiomatic expressions are ordinarily acquired only by much reading and conversation although questions about such matters may sometimes be answered by the dictionary. Dictionaries large enough to include quotations from standard authors are especially serviceable in determining questions of idiom."
The above quotation BEST supports the statement that idiomatic expressions
    A. give rise to meaningless arguments because they have no logical basis
    B. are widely used by recognized authors
    C. are explained in most dictionaries
    D. are more common in some languages than in others
    E. are best learned by observation of the language as actually used

38. "Individual differences in mental traits assume importance in fitting workers to jobs because such personal characteristics are persistent and are relatively little influenced by training and experience."
The above quotation BEST supports the statement that training and experience
   A. are limited in their effectiveness in fitting workers to jobs
   B. do not increase a worker's fitness for a job
   C. have no effect upon a person's mental traits
   D. have relatively little effect upon the individual's chances for success
   E. should be based on the mental traits of an individual

38.____

39. "The telegraph networks of the country now constitute wonderfully operated institutions, affording for ordinary use of modern, business an important means of communication. The transmission of message by electricity has reached the goal for which the postal service has long been striving, namely, the elimination of distance as an effective barrier of communication."
The above quotation BEST supports the statement that
   A. a new standard of communication has been attained
   B. in the telegraph service, messages seldom go astray
   C. it is the distance between the parties which creates the need for communication
   D. modern business relies more upon the telegraph than upon the mails
   E. the telegraph is a form of postal service

39.____

40. "The competition of buyers tends to keep prices up, the competition of sellers to send them down. Normally, the pressure of competition among sellers is stronger than that amount by buyers since the seller has his article to sell and must get rid of it, whereas the buyer is not committed to anything."
The above quotation BEST supports the statement that low prices are caused by
   A. buyer competition
   B. competition of buyers with sellers fluctuations in demand
   C. greater competition among sellers than among buyers
   D. more sellers than buyers

40.____

Questions 41-60.

DIRECTIONS: In answering Questions 41 through 60, find the CORRECT spelling of the word. Sometimes there is no correct spelling; if none of the suggested spellings is correct, indicate the letter D in the space at the right.

41. A. compitition   B. competition   41.____
    C. competetion   D. none of the above

42. A. diagnoesis   B. diagnossis   42.____
    C. diagnosis   D. none of the above

43. A. contenance   B. countenance   43.____
    C. countinance   D. none of the above

44. A. deliberate   B. deliberate   44.____
    C. deliberate   D. none of the above

45. A. knowlege   B. knolledge   45.____
    C. knowledge   D. none of the above

46. A. occassion   B. occasion   46.____
    C. ocassion   D. none of the above

47. A. sanctioned   B. sancktioned   47.____
    C. sanctionned   D. none of the above

48. A. predesessor   B. predecesar   48.____
    C. predecessor   D. none of the above

49. A. problemmatical B. problematical   49.____
    C. problematicle   D. none of the above

50. A. descendant   B. decendant   50.____
    C. desendant   D. none of the above

51. A. collapsible   B. collapseable   51.____
    C. collapseble   D. none of the above

52. A. sequance   B. sequence   52.____
    C. sequense   D. none of the above

53. A. obliterate   B. obbliterate   53.____
    C. obliterate   D. none of the above

54. A. ambigeuous   B. ambiguous   54.____
    C. ambiguous   D. none of the above

55. A. minieture   B. minneature   55.____
    C. miniature   D. none of the above

56. A. extemporaneous B. extempuraneus   56.____
    C. extemperaneous D. none of the above

57. A. hereditory   B. hereditary   57.____
    C. hereditairy   D. none of the above

58. A. conceivably   B. concieveably   58.____
    C. conceiveably   D. none of the above

59. A. extercate   B. extracate   59.____
    C. extricate   D. none of the above

60. A. auspiceous B. auspiseous
    C. auspicious D. none of the above   60.____

Questions 61-80.

DIRECTIONS: In answering Questions 61 through 80, select the sentence that is preferable with respect to grammar and usage such as would be suitable in a formal letter or report.

61. A. The receptionist must answer courteously the questions of all them callers.
    B. The questions of all callers had ought to be answered courteously.
    C. The receptionist must answer courteously the questions what are asked by the callers.
    D. There would have been no trouble if the receptionist had have always answered courteously.
    E. The receptionist should answer courteously the questions of all callers.   61.____

62. A. I had to learn a great number of rules, causing me to dislike the course.
    B. I disliked that study because it required the learning of numerous rules.
    C. I disliked that course very much, caused by the numerous rules I had to memorize.
    D. The cause of my dislike was on account of the numerous rules I had to learn in that course.
    E. The reason I disliked this study was because there were numerous rules that had to be learned.   62.____

63. A. If properly addressed, the letter will reach my mother and I.
    B. The letter had been addressed to myself and mother.
    C. I believe the letter was addressed to either my mother or I.
    D. My mother's name, as well as mine, was on the letter.
    E. If properly addressed, the letter it will reach either my mother or me.   63.____

64. A. A knowledge of commercial subjects and a mastery of English are essential if one wishes to be a good secretary.
    B. Two things necessary to a good secretary are the she should speak good English and too know commercial subjects.
    C. One cannot be a good secretary without she knows commercial subjects and English grammar.
    D. Having had god training in commercial subjects, the rules of English grammar should also be followed.
    E. A secretary seldom or ever succeeds without training in English as well as in commercial subjects.   64.____

65. A. He suspicions that the service is not so satisfactory as it should be.
    B. He believes that we should try and find whether the service is satisfactory.
    C. He raises the objection that the way which the service is given is not satisfactory.
    D. He believes that the quality of our services are poor.
    E. He believes that the service that we are giving is unsatisfactory.

65.____

66. A. Most all these statements have been supported by persons who are reliable and can be depended upon.
    B. The persons which have guaranteed these statements are reliable.
    C. Reliable persons guarantee the facts with regard to the truth of these statements.
    D. These statements can be depended on, for their truth has been guaranteed by reliable persons.
    E. Persons as reliable as what these are can be depended upon to make accurate statements.

66.____

67. A. Brown's & Company's employees have all been given increases in salary.
    B. Brown & Company recently increased the salaries of all its employees.
    C. Recently Brown & Company has increased their employees' salaries.
    D. Brown's & Company employees have recently received increases in salary.
    E. Brown & Company have recently increased the salaries of all its employees.

67.____

68. A. The personnel office has charge of employment, dismissals, and employee's welfare.
    B. Employment, together with dismissals and employees' welfare, are handled by the personnel department.
    C. The personnel office takes charge of employment, dismissals, and etc.
    D. The personnel office hires and dismisses employees, and their welfare is also its responsibility.
    E. The personnel office is responsible for the employment, dismissal, and welfare of employees.

68.____

69. A. This kind of pen is some better than that kind.
    B. I prefer having these pens than any other.
    C. This kind of pen is the most satisfactory for my use.
    D. In comparison with that kind of pen, this kind is more preferable.
    E. If I were to select between them all, I should pick this pen.

69.____

70. A. He could not make use of the report, as it was lacking of the needed information.
    B. This report was useless to him because there were no needed information in it.
    C. Since the report lacked the needed information, it was of no use to him.
    D. Being that the report lacked the needed information, he could not use it.
    E. Since the report did not contain the needed information, it was not real useful to him.

70.____

71. A. The paper we use for this purpose must be light, glossy, and stand hard usage as well.
    B. Only a light and a glossy, but durable, paper must be used for this purpose.
    C. For this purpose, we want a paper that is light, glossy, but that will stand hard wear.
    D. For this purpose, paper that is light, glossy, and durable is essential.
    E. Light and glossy paper, as well as standing hard usage, is necessary for this purpose.

71.____

72. A. The company had hardly declared the dividend till the notices were prepared for mailing.
    B. They had no sooner declared the dividend when they sent the notices to the stockholders.
    C. No sooner had the dividend been declared than the notices were prepared for mailing.
    D. Scarcely had the dividend been declared than the notices were sent out.
    E. The dividend had not scarcely been declared when the notices were ready for mailing.

72.____

73. A. Of all the employees, he spends the most time at the office.
    B. He spends more time at the office than that of his employees.
    C. His working hours are longer or at least equal to those of the other employees.
    D. He devotes as much, if not more, time to his work than the rest of the employees.
    E. He works the longest of any other employee in the office.

73.____

74. A. In the reports of typists' speeds, the job analyst found some records that are kind of unusual.
    B. It says in the job analyst's report that some employees type with great speed.
    C. The job analyst found that, in reviewing the typists' work Reports, that some unusual typing speeds had been made.
    D. Work reports showing typing speeds include some typists who are unusual.
    E. In reviewing the typists' work reports, the job analyst found records of unusual typing speeds.

74.____

75. A. It is quite possible that we shall reemploy anyone whose training fits them to do the work.
    B. It is probable that we shall reemploy those who have been trained to do the work.
    C. Such of our personnel that have been trained to do the work will be again employed.
    D. We expect to reemploy the ones who have had training enough that they can do the work.
    E. Some of these people have been trained.

75.____

76. A. He as well as his publisher were pleased with the success of the book.
    B. The success of the book pleased both his publisher and he.
    C. Both his publisher and he was pleased with the success of the book.
    D. Neither he or his publisher was disappointed with the success of the book.
    E. His publisher was as pleased as he with the success of the book.

77. A. You have got to get rid of some of these people if you expect to have the quality of the work improve
    B. The quality of the work would improve if they would leave fewer people do it.
    C. I believe it would be desirable to have fewer persons during this work.
    D. If you had planned on employing fewer people than this to do the work, this situation would not have arose.
    E. Seeing how you have all those people on that work, it is not surprising that you have a great deal of confusion.

78. A. She made lots of errors in her typed report, and which caused her to be reprimanded.
    B. The supervisor reprimanded the typist, whom she believed had made careless errors.
    C. Many errors were found in the report which she typed and could not disregard them.
    D. The typist would have corrected the errors, had she of known that the supervisor would see the report.
    E. The errors in the typed report were so numerous that they could hardly be overlooked.

79. A. This kind of a worker achieves success through patience.
    B. Success does not often come to men of this type except they who are patient.
    C. Because they are patient, these sort of workers usually achieve success.
    D. This worker has more patience than any man in his office.
    E. This kind of worker achieves success through patience.

80. A. I think that they will promote whoever has the best record.
    B. The firm would have liked to have promoted all employees with good records.
    C. Such of them that have the best records have excellent prospects of promotion.
    D. I feel sure they will give the promotion to whomever has the best record.
    E. Whoever they find to have the best record will, I think, be promoted.

KEY (CORRECT ANSWERS)

1. B	21. C	41. B	61. E
2. A	22. D	42. C	62. B
3. C	23. A	43. B	63. D
4. E	24. D	44. B	64. A
5. C	25. B	45. C	65. E
6. D	26. E	46. B	66. D
7. A	27. C	47. A	67. B
8. A	28. D	48. D	68. E
9. B	29. B	49. B	69. C
10. B	30. C	50. A	70. C
11. C	31. B	51. A	71. D
12. A	32. B	52. B	72. C
13. C	33. C	53. D	73. A
14. E	34. E	54. C	74. E
15. B	35. D	55. D	75. B
16. D	36. B	56. A	76. E
17. E	37. E	57. B	77. C
18. D	38. A	58. A	78. E
19. A	39. A	59. C	79. E
20. C	40. D	60. C	80. A

EXAMINATION SECTION
TEST 1

DIRECTIONS: Each question or incomplete statement is followed by several suggested answers or completions. Select the one that BEST answers the question or completes the statement. *PRINT THE LETTER OF THE CORRECT ANSWER IN THE SPACE AT THE RIGHT.*

Questions 1-22.

DIRECTIONS: Read through each group of words. Indicate in the space at the right the letter of the misspelled word.

1. A. miniature   B. recession   1._____
    C. accommodate   D. supress

2. A. mortgage   B. illogical   2._____
    C. fasinate   D. pronounce

3. A. calendar   B. heros   3._____
    C. ecstasy   D. librarian

4. A. initiative   B. extraordinary   4._____
    C. villian   D. exaggerate

5. A. absence   B. sense   5._____
    C. dosn't   D. height

6. A. curiosity   B. ninety   6._____
    C. truely   D. grammar

7. A. amateur   B. definate   7._____
    C. meant   D. changeable

8. A. excellent   B. studioes   8._____
    C. achievement   D. weird

9. A. goverment   B. description   9._____
    C. sergeant   D. desirable

10. A. proceed   B. anxious   10._____
    C. neice   D. precede

11. A. environment   B. omitted   11._____
    C. apparant   D. misconstrue

12. A. comparative   B. hindrance   12._____
    C. benefited   D. unamimous

13. A. embarrass   B. recommend   13.____
    C. desciple   D. argument

14. A. sophomore   B. suprintendent   14.____
    C. concievable D. disastrous

15. A. agressive   B. questionnaire   15.____
    C. occurred   D. rhythm

16. A. peaceable   B. conscientious   16.____
    C. redicule   D. deterrent

17. A. mischievious B. writing   17.____
    C. competition D. athletics

18. A. auxiliary   B. synonymous   18.____
    C. maneuver   D. repitition

19. A. existence   B. optomistic   19.____
    C. acquitted   D. tragedy

20. A. hypocrisy   B. parrallel   20.____
    C. exhilaration D. prevalent

21. A. convalesence B. infallible   21.____
    C. destitute   D. grotesque

22. A. magnanimity B. asassination   22.____
    C. incorrigible D. pestilence

Questions 23-40.

DIRECTIONS: In Questions 23 through 40, one sentence fragment contains an error in punctuation or capitalization. Indicate the letter of the INCORRECT sentence fragment and place it in the space at the right.

23. A. Despite a year's work   23.____
    B. in a well-equipped laboratory
    C. my Uncle failed to complete his research
    D. now he will never graduate.

24. A. Gene, if you are going to sleep   24.____
    B. all afternoon I will enter
    C. that ladies' golf tournament
    D. sponsored by the Chamber of Commerce.

25. A. Seeing the cat slink toward the barn,
    B. the farmer's wife jumped off the
    C. ladder picked up a broom, and began
    D. shouting at the top of her voice.

    25.____

26. A. Extending over southeast Idaho and
    B. northwest Wyoming, the Tetons
    C. are noted for their height; however the
    D. highest peak is actually under 14,000 feet.

    26.____

27. A. "Sarah, can you recall the name
    B. of the English queen
    C. who supposedly said, 'We are not
    D. amused?"

    27.____

28. A. My aunt's graduation present to me
    B. cost, I imagine more than she could
    C. actually afford. It's a
    D. Swiss watch with numerous features.

    28.____

29. A. On the left are examples of buildings
    B. from the Classical Period; two temples
    C. one of which was dedicated to Zeus; the
    D. Agora, a marketplace; and a large arch.

    29.____

30. A. Tired of sonic booms, the people who
    B. live near Springfield's Municipal Airport
    C. formed an anti noise organization
    D. with the amusing name of Sound Off.

    30.____

31. A. "Joe, Mrs. Sweeney said, "your family
    B. arrives Sunday. Since you'll be in
    C. the Labor Day parade, we could ask Mr.
    D. Krohn, who has a big car, to meet them."

    31.____

32. A. The plumber emerged from the basement and
    B. said, "Mr. Cohen I found the trouble in
    C. your water heater. Could you move those
    D. Schwinn bikes out of my way?"

    32.____

33. A. The President walked slowly to the
    B. podium, bowed to Edward Everett Hale
    C. the other speaker, and began his formal address:
    D. "Fourscore and seven years ago...."

    33.____

34. A. Mr. Fontana, I hope, will arrive before
    B. the beginning of the ceremonies; however,
    C. if his plane is delayed, I have a substitute
    D. speaker who can be here at a moments' notice.

    34.____

35. A. Gladys wedding dress, a satin creation,
    B. lay crumpled on the floor; her veil,
    C. torn and streaked, lay nearby. "Jilted!"
    D. shrieked Gladys. She was clearly annoyed.

35._____

36. A. Although it is poor grammar, the word
    B. hopefully has become television's newest
    C. pet expression; I hope (to use the correct
    D. form) that it will soon pass from favor.

36._____

37. A.   Plaza Apartment Hotel
    B.   103 Tower road
    C.   Hampstead, Iowa 52025
    D.   March 13, 2021

37._____

38. A. Circulation Department
    B. British History Illustrated
    C. 3000 Walnut Street
    D. Boulder Colorado 80302

38._____

39. A. Dear Sirs:
    B.   Last spring I ordered a subscription to your
    C. magazine. I had read and enjoyed the May
    D. issue containing the article titled "kings."

39._____

40. A.   I have not however, received a
    B. single issue. Will you check this?
    C.   Sincerely,
    D. Maria Herrera

40._____

Questions 41-70.

DIRECTIONS: Questions 41 through 70 represent common grammatical concerns: subject-verb agreement, appropriate use of pronouns, and appropriate use of verbs. Read each sentence and indicate the letter of the grammatically CORRECT answer in the space at the right.

41. THE REIVERS, one of William Faulkner's last works, _____ made into a movie starring Steve McQueen.
    A. has been   B. have been   C. are being   D. were

41._____

42. He _____ on the ground, his eyes fastened on an ant slowly pushing a morsel of food toward the ant hill.
    A. layed   B. laid   C. had laid   D. lay

42._____

43. Nobody in the tri-cities _____ to admit that a flood could be disastrous.
    A. are willing   B. have been willing
    C. is willing   D. were willing

43._____

44. "_____," the senator asked, "have you convinced to run against the incumbent?" 44._____
    A. Who   B. Whom   C. Whomever   D. Womsoever

45. Of all the psychology courses that I took, Statistics 101 _____ the most demanding. 45._____
    A. was   B. are   C. is   D. were

46. Neither the conductor nor the orchestra members _____ the music to be applauded so enthusiastically. 46._____
    A. were expecting   B. was expecting
    C. is expected   D. has been expecting

47. The requirements for admission to the Lettermen's Club _____ posted outside the athletic director's office for months. 47._____
    A. was   B. was being   C. has been   D. have been

48. Please give me a list of the people _____ to compete in the kayak race. 48._____
    A. whom you think have planned   B. who you think has planned
    C. who you think is planning   D. who you think are planning

49. I saw Eloise and Abelard earlier today; _____ were riding around in a fancy 1956 MG. 49._____
    A. she and him   B. her and him   C. she and he   D. her and he

50. If you _____ the trunk in the attic, I'll unpack it later today. 50._____
    A. can sit   B. are able to sit
    C. can set   D. have sat

51. _____ all of the flour been used, or may I borrow three cups? 51._____
    A. Have   B. Has   C. Is   D. Could

52. In exasperation, the cycle shop's owner suggested that _____ there too long. 52._____
    A. us boys were   B. we boys were
    C. us boys had been   D. we boys had been

53. Idleness as well as money _____ the root of all evil. 53._____
    A. have been   B. were to have been
    C. is   D. are

54. Only the string players from the quartet—Gregory, Isaac, _____—remained after the concert to answer questions. 54._____
    A. him, and I   B. he, and I
    C. him, and me   D. he, and me

55. Of all the antiques that _____ for sale, Gertrude chose to buy a stupid glass thimble. 55._____
    A. was   B. is
    C. would have   D. were

56. The detective snapped, "Don't confuse me with theories about _____ you believe committed the crime!"
    A. who B. whom C. whomever D. which

57. _____ when we first called, we might have avoided our present predicament.
    A. The plumber's coming
    B. If the plumber would have come
    C. If the plumber had come
    D. If the plumber was to have come

58. We thought the sun _____ in the north until we discovered that our compass was defective.
    A. had rose
    B. had risen
    C. had rised
    D. had raised

59. Each play of Shakespeare's _____ more than _____ share of memorable characters.
    A. contain its
    B. contains; its
    C. contains; it's
    D. contain; their

60. Our English teacher suggested to _____ seniors that either Tolstoy or Dickens _____ the outstanding novelist of the nineteenth century.
    A. we; was considered
    B. we; were considered
    C. us; was considered
    D. us; were considered

61. Sherlock Holmes, together with his great friend and companion Dr. Watson, _____ to aid the woman _____ had stumbled into the room.
    A. has agreed; who
    B. have agreed; whom
    C. has agreed; whom
    D. have agreed; who

62. Several of the deer _____ when they spotted my backpack _____ open in the meadow.
    A. was frightened; laying
    B. were frightened; lying
    C. were frightened; laying
    D. was frightened; lying

63. After the Scholarship Committee announces _____ selection, hysterics often _____.
    A. it's; occur
    B. its; occur
    C. their; occur
    D. their; occurs

64. I _____ the key on the table last night so you and _____ could find it.
    A. layed; her
    B. lay; she
    C. laid; she
    D. laid; her

65. Some of the antelope _____ wandered away from the meadow where the rancher _____ the block of salt.
    A. has; sat
    B. has; set
    C. have; had set
    D. has; sets

66. Macaroni and cheese _____ best to us (that is, to Andy and _____) when Mother adds extra cheddar cheese.
    A. tastes; I
    B. tastes; me
    C. taste; me
    D. taste; I

67. Frank said, "It must have been _____ called the phone company."
    A. she who
    B. she whom
    C. her who
    D. her whom

68. The herd _____ moving restlessly at every bolt of lightning; it was either Ted or _____ who saw the beginning of the stampede.
    A. was; me
    B. were; I
    C. was; I
    D. have been; me

69. The foreman _____ his lateness by saying that his alarm clock _____ until six minutes before eight.
    A. explains; had not rang
    B. explained; has not rung
    C. has explained; rung
    D. explained; hadn't rung

70. Of all the coaches, Ms. Cox is the only one who _____ that Sherry dives more gracefully than _____.
    A. is always saying; I
    B. is always saying; me
    C. are always saying; I
    D. were always saying; me

Questions 71-90.

DIRECTIONS: Choose the word in Questions 71 through 90 that is MOST opposite in meaning to the italicized word.

71. *fact*
    A. statistic
    B. statement
    C. incredible
    D. conjecture

72. *stiff*
    A. fastidious
    B. babble
    C. supple
    D. apprehensive

73. *blunt*
    A. concise
    B. tactful
    C. artistic
    D. humble

74. *foreign*
    A. pertinent
    B. comely
    C. strange
    D. scrupulous

75. *anger*
    A. infer
    B. pacify
    C. taint
    D. revile

76. *frank*
    A. earnest
    B. reticent
    C. post
    D. expensive

77. *secure*
    A. precarious   B. acquire   C. moderate   D. frenzied

78. *petty*
    A. harmonious   B. careful
    C. forthright   D. momentous

79. *concede*
    A. dispute   B. reciprocate
    C. subvert   D. propagate

80. *benefit*
    A. liquidation   B. bazaar
    C. detriment   D. profit

81. *capricious*
    A. preposterous   B. constant
    C. diabolical   D. careless

82. *boisterous*
    A. devious   B. valiant   C. girlish   D. taciturn

83. *harmony*
    A. congruence   B. discord   C. chagrin   D. melody

84. *laudable*
    A. auspicious   B. despicable
    C. acclaimed   D. doubtful

85. *adherent*
    A. partisan   B. stoic   C. renegade   D. recluse

86. *exuberant*
    A. frail   B. corpulent   C. austere   D. bigot

87. *spurn*
    A. accede   B. flail   C. efface   D. annihilate

88. *spontaneous*
    A. hapless   B. corrosive
    C. intentional   D. willful

89. *disparage*
    A. abolish   B. exude   C. incriminate   D. extol

90. *timorous*
    A. succinct   B. chaste   C. audacious   D. insouciant

KEY (CORRECT ANSWERS)

1. D	21. A	41. A	61. A	81. B
2. C	22. B	42. D	62.	82. D
3. B	23. C	43. C	63. B	83. B
4. C	24. B	44. B	64. C	84. B
5. C	25. C	45. A	65. C	85. C
6. C	26. C	46. A	66. B	86. C
7. B	27. D	47. D	67. A	87. A
8. B	28. B	48. A	68. C	88. C
9. A	29. B	49. C	69. D	89. D
10. C	30. C	50. C	70. A	90. C
11. C	31. A	51. B	71. D	
12. D	32. B	52. D	72. C	
13. C	33. B	53. C	73. B	
14. C	34. D	54. B	74. A	
15. A	35. A	55. D	75. B	
16. C	36. B	56. B	76. B	
17. A	37. B	57. C	77. A	
18. D	38. D	58. B	78. D	
19. B	39. D	59. B	79. A	
20. B	40. A	60. C	80. C	

READING COMPREHENSION
UNDERSTANDING AND INTERPRETING WRITTEN MATERIAL
EXAMINATION SECTION
TEST 1

DIRECTIONS: Each question or incomplete statement is followed by several suggested answers or completions. Select the one that BEST answers the question or completes the statement. *PRINT THE LETTER OF THE CORRECT ANSWER IN THE SPACE AT THE RIGHT.*

Questions 1-4.

DIRECTIONS: Questions 1 through 4 are to be answered SOLELY on the basis of the following paragraph.

An annual leave allowance, which combines leaves previously given for vacation, personal business, family illness, and other reasons shall be granted members. Calculation of credits for such leave shall be on an annual basis beginning January 1st of each year. Annual leave credits shall be based on time served by members during preceding calendar year. However, when credits have been accrued and member retires during current year, additional annual leave credits shall, in this instance, be granted at accrual rate of three days for each completed month of service, excluding terminal leave. If accruals granted for completed months of service extend into following month, member shall be granted an additional three days accrual for completed month. This shall be the only condition where accruals in a current year are granted for vacation period in such year.

1. According to the above paragraph, if a fireman's wife were to become seriously ill so that he would take time off from work to be with her, such time off would be deducted from his _____ leave allowance.
   A. annual
   B. vacation
   C. personal business
   D. family illness

2. Terminal leave means leave taken
   A. at the end of the calendar year
   B. at the end of the vacation year
   C. immediately before retirement
   D. before actually earned, because of an emergency

3. A fireman appointed on July 1, 2017 will be able to take his first full or normal annual leave during the period
   A. July 1, 2017 to June 30, 2018
   B. Jan. 1, 2018 to Dec. 31, 2018
   C. July 1, 2018 to June 30, 2019
   D. Jan. 1, 2019 to Dec. 31, 2019

4. According to the above paragraph, a member who retires on July 15 of this year will be entitled to receive leave allowance based on this year of _____ days.
   A. 15
   B. 18
   C. 22
   D. 24

5. Fire alarm boxes are electromechanical devices for transmitting a coded signal. In each box, there is a trainwork of wheels. When the box is operated, a spring-activated code wheel begins to revolve. The code number of the box is etched on the circumference of the code wheel, and the latter is associated with the circuit in such a way that when it revolves it causes the circuit to open and close in a predetermined manner, thereby transmitting its particular signal to the central station. A fire alarm box is nothing more than a device for interrupting the flow of current in a circuit in such a way as to produce a coded signal that may be decoded by the dispatchers in the central office.
Based on the above, select the FALSE statement.
   A. Each standard fire alarm box has its own code wheel.
   B. The code wheel operates when the box is pulled.
   C. The code wheel is operated electrically.
   D. Only the break in the circuit by the notched wheel causes the alarm signal to be transmitted to the central office.

Questions 6-9.

DIRECTIONS: Questions 6 through 9 are to be answered SOLELY on the basis of the following paragraph.

Ventilation, as used in firefighting operations, means opening up a building or structure in which a fire is burning to release the accumulated heat, smoke, and gases. Lack of knowledge of the principles of ventilation on the part of firemen may result in unnecessary punishment due to ventilation being neglected or improperly handled. While ventilation itself extinguishes no fires, when used in an intelligent manner, it allows firemen to get at the fire more quickly, easily, and with less danger and hardship.

6. According to the above paragraph, the MOST important result of failure to apply the principles of ventilation at a fire may be
   A. loss of public confidence   B. waste of water
   C. excessive use of equipment   D. injury to firemen

7. It may be inferred from the above paragraph that the CHIEF advantage of ventilation is that it
   A. eliminates the need for gas masks
   B. reduces smoke damage
   C. permits firemen to work closer to the fire
   D. cools the fire

8. Knowledge of the principles of ventilation, as defined in the above paragraph, would be LEAST important in a fire in a
   A. tenement house   B. grocery store
   C. ship's hold   D. lumberyard

9. We may conclude from the above paragraph that for the well-trained and equipped fireman, ventilation is
   A. a simple matter   B. rarely necessary
   C. relatively unimportant D. a basic tool

Questions 10-13.

DIRECTIONS: Questions 10 through 13 are to be answered SOLELY on the basis of the following passage.

Fire exit drills should be established and held periodically to effectively train personnel to leave their working area promptly upon proper signal and to evacuate the building, speedily but without confusion. All fire exit drills should be carefully planned and carried out in a serious manner under rigid discipline so as to provide positive protection in the event of a real emergency. As a general rule, the local fire department should be furnished advance information regarding the exact date and time the exit drill is scheduled. When it is impossible to hold regular drills, written instructions should be distributed to all employees.

Depending upon individual circumstances, fires in warehouses vary from those of fast development that are almost instantly beyond any possibility of employee control to others of relatively slow development where a small readily attackable flame may be present for periods of time up to 15 minutes or more during which simple attack with fire extinguishers or small building hoses may prevent the fire development. In any case, it is characteristic of many warehouse fires that at a certain point in development they flash up to the top of the stack, increase heat quickly, and spread rapidly. There is a degree of inherent danger in attacking warehouse type fires, and all employees should be thoroughly trained in the use of the types of extinguishers or small hoses in the buildings and well instructed in the necessity of always staying between the fire and a direct pass to an exit.

10. Employees should be instructed that, when fighting a fire, they MUST
    A. try to control the blaze
    B. extinguish any fire in 15 minutes
    C. remain between the fire and a direct passage to the exit
    D. keep the fire between themselves and the fire exit

11. Whenever conditions are such that regular fire drills cannot be held, then which one of the following actions should be taken?
    A. The local fire department should be notified.
    B. Rigid discipline should be maintained during work hours.
    C. Personnel should be instructed to leave their working area by whatever means are available.
    D. Employees should receive fire drill procedures in writing.

12. The above passage indicates that the purpose of fire exit drills is to train employees to
    A. control a fire before it becomes uncontrollable
    B. act as firefighters
    C. leave the working area promptly
    D. be serious

13. According to the above passage, fire exit drills will prove to be of UTMOST effectiveness if
    A. employee participation is made voluntary
    B. they take place periodically
    C. the fire department actively participates
    D. they are held without advance planning

Questions 14-16.

DIRECTIONS: Questions 14 through 16 are to be answered SOLELY on the basis of the following paragraph.

The heat output from unit heaters will depend on how fast and how completely dry hot steam fills the unit core. For complete and fast air removal and rapid drainage of condensate, use a trap actuated by water or vapor (inverted bucket trap) and not a trap operated by temperature only (thermostatic or bellows trap). A temperature-actuated trap will hold back the hot condensate until it cools to a point where the thermal element opens. When this happens, the condensate backs up in the heater and reduces the heat output. With a water-actuated trap, this will not happen as the water or condensate is discharged as fast as it is formed.

14. On the basis of the information given in the above paragraph, it can be concluded that the PROPER type of trap to use for a unit heater is a(n) _____ trap.
    A. thermostatic
    B. bellows-type
    C. inverted bucket
    D. temperature

15. According to the above paragraph, the MAIN reason for using the type of trap specified for a unit heater is to
    A. bring the condensate up to steam temperature
    B. prevent reduction in the heat output of the unit heater
    C. permit cycling of the heater
    D. maintain constant temperature of condensate in the trap

16. As used in the above paragraph, the word *actuated* means MOST NEARLY
    A. clogged   B. operated   C. cleaned   D. vented

Questions 17-25.

DIRECTIONS: Questions 17 through 25 are to be answered SOLELY on the basis of the following passage. Each question consists of a statement. You are to indicate whether the statement is TRUE (T) or FALSE (F).

MOVING AN OFFICE

An office with all its equipment is sometimes moved during working hours. This is a difficult task and must be done in an orderly manner to avoid confusion. The operation should be planned in such a way as not to interrupt the progress of work usually done in the office and to make possible the accurate placement of the furniture and records in the new location. If the office moves to a place inside the same building, the desks and files are moved with all their contents. If the movement is to another building, the contents of each desk and file are placed in boxes. Each box is marked with a letter showing the particular section in the new quarters to which it is to be moved. Also marked on each box is the number of the desk or file on which the box is to be placed. Each piece of equipment must have a numbered tag. The number of each piece of equipment is put in soft chalk on the floor in the new office to show the proper location, and several floor plans are made to show where each piece of equipment goes. When the moving is done, someone is stationed at each of the several exits of the old office to see that each box or piece of equipment has its destination clearly marked on it. At the new office, someone stands at each of the several entrances with a copy of the floor plan and directs the placing of the furniture and equipment according to the floor plan. No one should interfere at this point with the arrangements shown on the plan. Improvements in arrangement can be considered and made at a later date.

17. It is a hard job to move an office from one place to another during working hours. 17.____

18. Confusion cannot be avoided if an office is moved during working hours. 18.____

19. The work usually done in an office must be stopped for the day when the office is moved during working hours. 19.____

20. If an office is moved from one floor to another in the same building, the contents of a desk are taken out and put into boxes for moving. 20.____

21. If boxes are used to hold material from desks when moving an office, the box is numbered the same as the desk on which it is to be put. 21.____

22. Letters are marked in soft chalk on the floor at the new quarters to show where the desks should go when moved. 22.____

23. When the moving begins, a person is put at each exit of the old office to check that each box and piece of equipment has clearly marked on it where to go. 23.____

24. A person stationed at each entrance of the new quarters to direct the placing of the furniture and equipment has a copy of the floor plan of the new quarters. 24.____

25. If, while the furniture is being moved into the new office, a person helping at a doorway gets an idea of a better way to arrange the furniture, he should change the planned arrangement and make a record of the change. 25.____

KEY (CORRECT ANSWERS)

1.	A		11.	D
2.	C		12.	C
3.	D		13.	B
4.	B		14.	C
5.	C		15.	B
6.	D		16.	B
7.	C		17.	T
8.	D		18.	F
9.	D		19.	F
10.	C		20.	F

21. T
22. F
23. T
24. T
25. F

TEST 2

DIRECTIONS: Each question or incomplete statement is followed by several suggested answers or completions. Select the one that BEST answers the question or completes the statement. *PRINT THE LETTER OF THE CORRECT ANSWER IN THE SPACE AT THE RIGHT.*

Questions 1-4.

DIRECTIONS: Questions 1 through 4 are to be answered SOLELY on the basis of the following paragraph.

In all cases of homicide, members of the Police Department who investigate will make every effort to obtain statements from dying persons. Such statements are of the greatest importance to the District Attorney. In many cases, there may be a failure to solve the crime if they are not taken. The principal element to be considered in taking the declaration of a dying person is his mental attitude. In order to be admissible in evidence, the person must have no hope of recovery. The patient will be fully interrogated on that point before a statement is taken.

1. In cases of homicide, according to the above paragraph, members of the police force will
    A. try to change the mental attitude of the dying person
    B. attempt to obtain a statement from the dying person
    C. not give the information they obtain directly to the District Attorney
    D. be careful not to injure the dying person unnecessarily

1.____

2. The mental attitude of the person making the dying statement is of GREAT importance because it can determine, according to the above paragraph, whether the
    A. victim should be interrogated in the presence of witnesses
    B. victim will be willing to make a statement of any kind
    C. statement will tell the District Attorney who committed the crime
    D. the statement can be used as evidence

2.____

3. District Attorneys find that statements of a dying person are important, according to the above paragraph, because
    A. it may be that the victim will recover and then refuse to testify
    B. they are important elements in determining the mental attitude of the victim
    C. they present a point of view
    D. it may be impossible to punish the criminal without such a statement

3.____

4. A well-known gangster is found dying from a bullet wound. The patrolman first on the scene, in the presence of witnesses, tells the man that he is going to die and asks, *Who shot you?* The gangster says, *Jones shot me, but he hasn't killed me. I'll live to get him.* He then falls back dead.
According to the above paragraph, this statement is
    A. *admissible* in evidence; the man was obviously speaking the truth
    B. *not admissible* in evidence; the man obviously did not believe that he was dying

4.____

C. *admissible* in evidence; there were witnesses to the statement
D. *not admissible* in evidence; the victim did not sign any statement and the evidence is merely hearsay

Questions 5-7.

DIRECTIONS: Questions 5 through 7 are to be answered SOLELY on the basis of the following paragraph.

The factors contributing to crime and delinquency are varied and complex. The home and its immediate environment have been found to be crucial in determining the behavior patterns of the individual, and criminality can frequently be traced to faulty family relationships and a bad neighborhood. But in the search for a clearer understanding of the underlying causes of delinquent and criminal behavior, the total environment must be taken into consideration.

5. According to the above paragraph, family relationships
   A. tend to become faulty in bad neighborhoods
   B. are important in determining the actions of honest people as well as criminals
   C. are the only important element in the understanding of causes of delinquency
   D. are determined by the total environment

6. According to the above paragraph, the causes of crime and delinquency are
   A. not simple   B. not meaningless
   C. meaningless   D. simple

7. According to the above paragraph, faulty family relationships FREQUENTLY are
   A. responsible for varied and complex results
   B. caused when one or both parents have a criminal behavior pattern
   C. independent of the total environment
   D. the cause of criminal acts

Questions 8-10.

DIRECTIONS: Questions 8 through 10 are to be answered SOLELY on the basis of the following paragraph.

A change in the specific problems which confront the police and in the methods for dealing with them has taken place in the last few decades. The automobile is a two-way symbol of this change in policing. It menaces every city with a complicated traffic problem and has speeded up the process of committing a crime and making a getaway, but at the same time has increased the effectiveness of police operations. However, the major concern of police departments continues to be the antisocial or criminal actions and behavior of human beings.

8. On the basis of the above paragraph, it can be stated that, for the most part, in the past few decades the specific problems of a police force
   A. have changed but the general problems have not
   B. as well as the general problems have changed
   C. have remained the same but the general problems have changed
   D. as well as the general problems have remained the same

8.____

9. According to the above paragraph, advances in science and industry have, in general, made the police
   A. operations less effective from the overall point of view
   B. operations more effective from the overall point of view
   C. abandon older methods of solving police problems
   D. concern themselves more with the antisocial acts of human beings

9.____

10. The automobile is a *two-way symbol*, according to the above paragraph, because its use
    A. has speeded up getting to and away from the scene of a crime
    B. both helps and hurts police operations
    C. introduces a new antisocial act—traffic violation—and does away with criminals like horse thieves
    D. both increases and decreases speed by introducing traffic problems

10.____

Questions 11-14.

DIRECTIONS: Questions 11 through 14 are to be answered SOLELY on the basis of the following passage on INSTRUCTIONS TO COIN AND TOKEN CASHIERS.

INSTRUCTIONS TO COIN AND TOKEN CASHIERS

Cashiers should reset the machine registers to an even starting number before commencing the day's work. Money bags received directly from collecting agents shall be counted and receipted for on the collecting agent's form. Each cashier shall be responsible for all coin or token bags accepted by him. He must examine all bags to be used for bank deposits for cuts and holes before placing them in use. Care must be exercised so that bags are not cut in opening them. Each bag must be opened separately and verified before another bag is opened. The machine register must be cleared before starting the count of another bag. The amount shown on the machine register must be compared with the amount on the bag tag. The empty bag must be kept on the table for re-examination should there be a difference between the amount on the bag tag and the amount on the machine register.

11. A cashier should BEGIN his day's assignment by
    A. counting and accepting all money bags
    B. resetting the counting machine register
    C. examining all bags for cuts and holes
    D. verifying the contents of all money bags

11.____

12. In verifying the amount of money in the bags received from the collecting agent, it is BEST to
    A. check the amount in one bag at a time
    B. base the total on the amount on the collecting agent's form
    C. repeat the total shown on the bag tag
    D. refer to the bank deposit receipt

12.____

13. A cashier is instructed to keep each empty coin bag on his table while verifying its contents CHIEFLY because, as long as the bag is on the table
    A. it cannot be misplaced
    B. the supervisor can see how quickly the cashier works
    C. cuts and holes are easily noticed
    D. a recheck is possible in case the machine count disagrees with the bag tag total

13.____

14. The INSTRUCTIONS indicate that it is NOT proper procedure for a cashier to
    A. assume that coin bags are free of cuts and holes
    B. compare the machine register total with the total shown on the bag tag
    C. sign a form when he receives coin bags
    D. reset the machine register before starting the day's counting

14.____

Questions 15-17.

DIRECTIONS: Questions 15 through 17 are to be answered SOLELY on the basis of the following passage.

The mass media are an integral part of the daily life of virtually every American. Among these media the youngest, television, is the most pervasive. Ninety-five percent of American homes have at least one T.V. set, and on the average that set is in use for about 40 hours each week. The central place of television in American life makes this medium the focal point of a growing national concern over the effects of media portrayals of violence on the values, attitudes, and behavior of an ever-increasing audience.

In our concern about violence and its causes, it is easy to make television a scapegoat. But we emphasize the fact that there is no simple answer to the problem of violence—no single explanation of its causes, and no single prescription for its control. It should be remembered that America also experienced high levels of crime and violence in periods before the advent of television.

The problem of balance, taste and artistic merit in entertaining programs on television are complex. We cannot <u>countenance</u> government censorship of television. Nor would we seek to impose arbitrary limitations on programming which might jeopardize television's ability to deal in dramatic presentations with controversial social issues. Nonetheless, we are deeply troubled by television's constant portrayal of violence, not in any genuine attempt to focus artistic expression on the human condition, but rather in pandering to a public preoccupation with violence that television itself has helped to generate,

15. According to the above passage, television uses violence MAINLY
    A. to highlight the reality of everyday existence
    B. to satisfy the audience's hunger for destructive action

15.____

C. to shape the values and attitudes of the public
D. when it films documentaries concerning human conflict

16. Which one of the following statements is BEST supported by the above passage? 16.____
    A. Early American history reveals a crime pattern which is not related to television.
    B. Programs should give presentations of social issues and never portray violent acts.
    C. Television has proven that entertainment programs can easily make the balance between taste and artistic merit a simple matter.
    D. Values and behavior should be regulated by governmental censorship.

17. Of the following, which word has the same meaning as *countenance*, as used in the above passage? 17.____
    A. Approve   B. Exhibit   C. Oppose   D. Reject

Questions 18-21.

DIRECTIONS: Questions 18 through 21 are to be answered SOLELY on the basis of the following passage.

Maintenance of leased or licensed areas on public parks or land has always been a problem. A good rule to follow in the administration and maintenance of such areas is to limit the responsibility of any lessee or licensee to the maintenance of the structures and grounds essential to the efficient operation of the concession, not including areas for the general use of the public, such as picnic areas, public comfort stations, etc.; except where such facilities are leased to another public agency or where special conditions make such inclusion practicable, and where a good standard of maintenance can be assured and enforced. If local conditions and requirements are such that public use areas are included, adequate safeguards to the public should be written into contracts and enforced in their administration, to insure that maintenance by the concessionaire shall be equal to the maintenance standards for other park property.

18. According to the above passage, when an area on a public park is leased to a concessionaire, it is usually BEST to 18.____
    A. confine the responsibility of the concessionaire to operation of the facilities and leave the maintenance function to the park agency
    B. exclude areas of general public use from the maintenance obligation of the concessionaire
    C. make the concessionaire responsible for maintenance of the entire area including areas of general public use
    D. provide additional comfort station facilities for the area

19. According to the above passage, a valid reason for giving a concessionaire responsibility for maintenance of a picnic area within his leased area is that 19.____
    A. local conditions and requirements make it practicable
    B. more than half of the picnic area falls within his leased area
    C. the concessionaire has leased picnic facilities to another public agency
    D. the picnic area falls entirely within his leased area

20. According to the above passage, a precaution that should be taken when a concessionaire is made responsible for maintenance of an area of general public use in a park is
    A. making sure that another public agency has not previously been made responsible for this area
    B. providing the concessionaire with up-to-date equipment, if practicable
    C. requiring that the concessionaire take out adequate insurance for the protection of the public
    D. writing safeguards to the public into the contract

20.____

KEY (CORRECT ANSWERS)

1.	B	11.	B
2.	D	12.	A
3.	D	13.	D
4.	B	14.	A
5.	B	15.	B
6.	A	16.	A
7.	D	17.	A
8.	A	18.	B
9.	B	19.	A
10.	B	20.	D

TEST 3

DIRECTIONS: Each question or incomplete statement is followed by several suggested answers or completions. Select the one that BEST answers the question or completes the statement. *PRINT THE LETTER OF THE CORRECT ANSWER IN THE SPACE AT THE RIGHT.*

Questions 1-5.

DIRECTIONS: Questions 1 through 5 are to be answered SOLELY on the basis of the following paragraph.

    Physical inspections are an important tool for the examiner because he will have to decide the case in many instances on the basis of the inspection report. Most proceedings in a rent office are commenced by the filing of a written application or complaint by an interested party; that is, either the landlord or the tenant. Such an application or complaint must be filed in duplicate in order that the opposing party may be served with a copy of the application or complaint and thus be given an opportunity to answer and oppose it. Sometimes, a further opportunity is given the applicant to file a written rebuttal or reply to his adversary's answer. Often an examiner can make a determination or decision based on the written application, the answer, and the reply to the answer; and, of course, it would speed up operations if it were always possible to make decisions based on written documents only. Unfortunately, decisions can't always be made that way. There are numerous occasions where disputed issues of fact remain which cannot be resolved on the basis of the written statements of the parties. Typical examples are the following: The tenant claims that the refrigerator or stove or bathroom fixture is not functioning properly and the landlord denies this It is obvious that in such cases an inspection of the accommodations is almost the only means of resolving such disputed issues,

1. According to the above paragraph,
    A. physical inspections are made in all cases
    B. physical inspections are seldom made
    C. it is sometimes possible to determine the facts in a case without a physical inspection
    D. physical inspections are made when it is necessary to verify the examiner's determination

2. According to the above paragraph, in MOST cases, proceedings are started by a(n)
    A. inspector discovering a violation
    B. oral complaint by a tenant or landlord
    C. request from another agency, such as the Building Department
    D. written complaint by a tenant or landlord

3. According to the above paragraph, when a tenant files an application with the rent office, the landlord is
    A. not told about the proceeding until after the examiner makes his determination
    B. given the duplicate copy of the application

1.____

2.____

3.____

C. notified by means of an inspector visiting the premises
D. not told about the proceeding until after the inspector has visited the premises

4. As used in the above paragraph, the word *disputed* means MOST NEARLY
   A. unsettled   B. contested   C. definite   D. difficult

5. As used in the above paragraph, the word *resolved* means MOST NEARLY
   A. settled   B. fixed   C. helped   D. amended

Questions 6-10.

DIRECTIONS: Questions 6 through 10 are to be answered SOLELY on the basis of the following paragraph.

The examiner should order or request an inspection of the housing accommodations. His request for a physical inspection should be in writing, identify the accommodations and the landlord and the tenant, and specify precisely just what the inspector is to look for and report on. Unless this request is specific and lists in detail every item which the examiner wishes to be reported, the examiner will find that the inspection has not served its purpose and that even with the inspector's report, he is still in no position to decide the case due to loose ends which have not been completely tied up. The items that the examiner is interested in should be separately numbered on the inspection request and the same number referred to in the inspector's report. You can see what it would mean if an inspector came back with a report that did not cover everything. It may mean a tremendous waste of time and often require a re-inspection.

6. According to the above paragraph, the inspector makes an inspection on the order of
   A. the landlord
   B. the tenant
   C. the examiner
   D. both the landlord and the tenant

7. According to the above paragraph, the reason for numbering each item that an inspector reports on is so that
   A. the report is neat
   B. the report can be easily read and referred to
   C. none of the examiner's requests for information is missed
   D. the report will be specific

8. The one of the following items that is NOT necessarily included in the request for inspection is
   A. location of dwelling
   B. name of landlord
   C. item to be checked
   D. type of building

9. As used in the above paragraph, the word *precisely* means MOST NEARLY
   A. exactly   B. generally   C. usually   D. strongly

10. As used in the above paragraph, the words *in detail* mean MOST NEARLY
    A. clearly   B. item by item   C. substantially   D. completely

Questions 11-13.

DIRECTIONS: Questions 11 through 13 are to be answered SOLELY on the basis of the following passage.

The agreement under which a tenant rents property from a landlord is known as a lease. Generally speaking, leases are classified as either short-term or long-term in duration. They are further subdivided according to the method used to determine the amount of periodic rent payments. Of the following types of lease in use, the more commonly used ones are the following:
1. The straight or fixed lease is one in which rent may be paid in equal amounts throughout the duration of the lease. These are usually restricted to short-term leasing, or somewhat longer-term if clauses in the lease provide for periodic escalation of payments as the economy shifts.
2. Percentage leasing, used for short-term commercial leasing, provides the landlord with a stipulated percentage of a tenant's gross sales from goods and services sold on the premises, in addition to a fixed amount of rent.
3. The net lease, generally long-term (ten years or more), requires the tenant to pay all operating costs, including real estate taxes and insurance. In a net-net lease, the tenant further agrees to meet mortgage interest and principal payments.
4. An escalated lease, which is a long-term lease, requires rent to be of a stipulated base amount which periodically is subject to escalation in accordance with cost-of-living index scales, or in direct proportion to taxes, insurance, and operating costs.

11. Based on the information given in the passage, which type of lease is MOST likely to be advantageous to a landlord if there is a high rate of inflation? _____ lease.
 A. Fixed B. Percentage C. Net D. Escalated

12. On the basis of thee above passage, which types of lease would generally be MOST suitable for a well-established textile company which requires permanent facilities for its large operations?
_____ lease and _____ lease.
 A. Percentage; escalated B. Escalated; net
 C. Straight; net D. Straight; percentage

13. According to the above passage, the ONLY type of lease which assures the same amount of rent throughout a specified interval is the _____ lease.
 A. straight B. percentage C. net-net D. escalated

Questions 14-15.

DIRECTIONS: Questions 14 and 15 are to be answered SOLELY on the basis of the following passage.

If you like people, if you seek contact with them rather than hide yourself in a corner, if you study your fellow men sympathetically, if you try consistently to contribute something to their success and happiness, if you are reasonably generous with your thought and your time, if you have a partial reserve with everyone but a seeming reserve with no one, you will get along with your superiors, your subordinates, and the human race.

By the scores of thousands, precepts and platitudes have been written for the guidance of personal conduct. The odd part of it is that, despite all of this labor, most of the frictions in modern society arise from the individual's feeling of inferiority, his false pride, his vanity, his unwillingness to yield space to any other man and his consequent urge to throw his own weight around. Goethe said that the quality which best enables a man to renew his own life, in his relation to others, is his capability of renouncing particular things at the right moment in order warmly to embrace something new in the next.

14. On the basis of the above passage, it may be INFERRED that
    A. a person should be unwilling to renounce privileges
    B. a person should realize that loss of a desirable job assignment may come at an opportune moment
    C. it is advisable for a person to maintain a considerable amount of reserve in his relationship with unfamiliar people
    D. people should be ready to contribute generously to a worthy charity

15. Of the following, the MOST valid implication made by the above passage is that
    A. a wealthy person who spends a considerable amount of money entertaining his friends is not really getting along with them
    B. if a person studies his fellow men carefully and impartially, he will tend to have good relationships with them
    C. individuals who maintain seemingly little reserve in their relationships with people have in some measure overcome their own feelings of inferiority
    D. most precepts that have been written for the guidance of personal conduct in relationships with other people are invalid

Questions 16-17.

DIRECTIONS: Questions 16 and 17 are to be answered SOLELY on the basis of the following passage.

When a design for a new bank note of the Federal Government has been prepared by the Bureau of Engraving and Printing and has been approved by the Secretary of the Treasury, the engravers begin the work of cutting the design in steel. No one engraver does all the work. Each man is a specialist. One works only on portraits, another on lettering, another on scroll work, and so on. Each engraver, with a steel tool known as a graver, and aided by a powerful magnifying glass, carefully carves his portion of the design into the steel. He knows that one false cut or a slip of his tool, or one miscalculation of width or depth of line, may destroy the merit of his work. A single mistake means that months or weeks of labor will have been in vain. The bureau is proud of the fact that no counterfeiter ever has duplicated the excellent work of its expert engravers.

16. According to the above passage, each engraver in the Bureau of Engraving and Printing
    A. must be approved by the Secretary of the Treasury before he can begin work on the design for a new bank note
    B. is responsible for engraving a complete design of a new bank note by himself
    C. designs new bank notes and submits them for approval to the Secretary of the Treasury
    D. performs sonly a specific part of the work of engraving a design for a new bank note

17. According to the above passage,
    A. an engraver's tools are not available to a counterfeiter
    B. mistakes made in engraving a design can be corrected immediately with little delay in the work of the Bureau
    C. the skilled work of the engravers has not been successfully reproduced by counterfeiter
    D. careful carving and cutting by the engraver is essential to prevent damage to equipment

Questions 18-21.

DIRECTIONS: Questions 18 through 21 are to be answered SOLELY on the basis of the following passage.

In the late fifties, the average American housewife spent $4.50 per day for a family of four on food and 5.15 hours in food preparation, if all of her food was *home prepared*; she spent $5.80 per day and 3.245 hours if all of her food was purchased *partially prepared*; and $6.70 per day and 1.64 hours if all of her food was purchased *ready-to-serve*.

Americans spent about 20 billion dollars for food products in 1941. They spent nearly 70 billion dollars in 1958. They spent 25 percent of their cash income on food in 1958. For the same kinds and quantities of food that consumers bought in 1941, they would have spent only 16% of their cash income in 1958. It is obvious that our food does cost more. Many factors contribute to this increase besides the additional cost that might be attributed to processing. Consumption of more expensive food items, higher marketing margins, and more food eaten in restaurants are other factors.

The Census of Manufacturers gives some indication of the total bill for processing. The value added by manufacturing of food and kindred products amounted to 3.5 billion of the 20 billion dollars spent for food in 1941. In the year 1958, the comparable figure had climbed to 14 billion dollars.

18. According to the above passage, the cash income of Americans in 1958 was MOST NEARLY _____ billion dollars.
    A. 11.2   B. 17.5   C. 70   D. 280

19. According to the above passage, if Americans bought the same kinds and quantities of food in 1958 as they did in 1941, they would have spent MOST NEARLY _____ billion dollars.
    A. 20   B. 45   C. 74   D. 84

20. According to the above passage, the percent increase in money spent for food in 1958 over 1941, as compared with the percentage increase in money spent for food processing in the same years,
    A. was greater
    B. was less
    C. was the same
    D. cannot be determined from the passage

21. In 1958, an American housewife who bought all of her food ready-to-serve saved time, as compared with the housewife who prepared all of her food at home
    A. 1.6 hours daily
    B. 1.9 hours daily
    C. 3.5 hours daily
    D. an amount of time which cannot be determined from the above passage

Questions 22-25.

DIRECTIONS: Questions 22 through 25 are to be answered SOLELY on the basis of the following passage.

Any member of the retirement system who is in city service, who files a proper application for service credit and agrees to deductions from his compensation at triple his normal rate of contribution, shall be credited with a period of city service previous to the beginning of his present membership in the retirement system. The period of service credited shall be equal to the period throughout which such triple deductions are made, but may not exceed the total of the city service the number rendered between his first day of eligibility for membership in the retirement system and the day he last became a member. After triple contributions for all of the first three years of service credit claimed, the remaining service credit may be purchased by a single payment of the sum of the remaining payments. If the total time purchasable exceeds ten years, triple contributions may be made for one-half of such time, and the remaining time purchased by a single payment of the sum of the remaining payments. Credit for service acquired in the above manner may be used only in determining the amount of any retirement benefit. Eligibility for such benefit will, in all cases, be based upon service rendered after the employee's membership last began, and will be exclusive of service credit purchased as described above.

22. According to the above passage, in order to obtain credit for city service previous to the beginning of an employee's present membership in the retirement system, the employee must
    A. apply for the service credit and consent to additional contributions to the retirement system
    B. apply for the service credit before he renews his membership in the retirement system
    C. have previous city service which does not exceed ten years
    D. make contributions to the retirement system for three years

23. According to the information in the above passage, credit for city service previous to the beginning of an employee's present membership in the retirement system is 23.____
    A. credited up to a maximum of ten years
    B. credited to any member of the retirement system
    C. used in determining the amount of the employee's benefits
    D. used in establishing the employee's eligibility to receive benefits

24. According to the information in the above passage, a member of the retirement system may purchase service credit for 24.____
    A. the period of time between his first day of eligibility for membership in the retirement system and the date he applies for the service credit
    B. one-half of the total of his previous city service if the total time exceeds ten years
    C. the period of time throughout which triple deductions are made
    D. the period of city service between his first day of eligibility for membership in the retirement system and the day he last became a member

25. Suppose that a member of the retirement system has filed an application for service credit for five years of previous city service. 25.____
    Based on the information in the above passage, the employee may purchase credit for this previous city service by making
    A. triple contributions for three years
    B. triple contributions for one-half of the time and a single payment of the sum of the remaining payments
    C. triple contributions for three years and a single payment of the sum of the remaining payments
    D. a single payment of the sum of the payments

KEY (CORRECT ANSWERS)

1. C
2. D
3. B
4. B
5. A

6. C
7. C
8. D
9. A
10. B

11. D
12. B
13. A
14. B
15. C

16. D
17. C
18. D
19. B
20. B

21. C
22. A
23. C
24. D
25. C

CLERICAL ABILITIES TEST
EXAMINATION SECTION
TEST 1

DIRECTIONS: Each question or incomplete statement is followed by several suggested answers or completions. Select the one that BEST answers the question or completes the statement. *PRINT THE LETTER OF THE CORRECT ANSWER IN THE SPACE AT THE RIGHT.*

Questions 1-10.

DIRECTIONS: Questions 1 through 10 consist of lines of names, dates, and numbers. For each question, you are to choose the option (A, B, C, or D) in Column II which EXACTLY matches the information in Column I. *PRINT THE LETTER OF THE CORRECT ANSWER IN THE SPACE AT THE RIGHT.*

SAMPLE QUESTION

Column I
Schneider 11/16/75 581932

Column II
A. Schneider 11/16/75 518932
B. Schneider 11/16/75 581932
C. Schnieder 11/16/75 581932
D. Shnieder 11/16/75 518932

The correct answer is B. Only Option B shows the name, date, and number exactly as they are in Column I. Option A has a mistake in the number. Option C has a mistake in the name. Option D has a mistake in the name and in the number. Now answer Questions 1 through 10 in the same manner.

Column I
1. Johnston 12/26/74 659251

   Column II
   A. Johnson 12/23/74 659251
   B. Johston 12/26/74 659251
   C. Johnston 12/26/74 695251
   D. Johnston 12/26/74 659251

   1.____

2. Allison 1/26/75 9939256

   A. Allison 1/26/75 9939256
   B. Alisson 1/26/75 9939256
   C. Allison 1/26/76 9399256
   D. Allison 1/26/75 9993356

   2.____

3. Farrell 2/12/75 361251

   A. Farell 2/21/75 361251
   B. Farrell 2/12/75 361251
   C. Farrell 2/21/75 361251
   D. Farrell 2/12/75 361151

   3.____

4. Guerrero 4/28/72 105689
    A. Guererro 4/28/72 105689
    B. Guererro 4/28/72 105986
    C. Guerrero 4/28/72 105869
    D. Guerrero 4/28/72 105689

4.____

5. McDonnell 6/05/73 478215
    A. McDonnell 6/15/73 478215
    B. McDonnell 6/05/73 478215
    C. McDonnell 6/05/73 472815
    D. MacDonell 6/05/73 478215

5.____

6. Shepard 3/31/71 075421
    A. Sheperd 3/31/71 075421
    B. Shepard 3/13/71 075421
    C. Shepard 3/31/71 075421
    D. Shepard 3/13/71 075241

6.____

7. Russell 4/01/69 031429
    A. Russell 4/01/69 031429
    B. Russell 4/10/69 034129
    C. Russell 4/10/69 031429
    D. Russell 4/01/69 034129

7.____

8. Phillips 10/16/68 961042
    A. Philipps 10/16/68 961042
    B. Phillips 10/16/68 960142
    C. Phillips 10/16/68 961042
    D. Philipps 10/16/68 916042

8.____

9. Campbell 11/21/72 624856
    A. Campbell 11/21/72 624856
    B. Campbell 11/21/72 624586
    C. Campbell 11/21/72 624686
    D. Campbel 11/21/72 624856

9.____

10. Patterson 9/18/71 76199176
    A. Patterson 9/18/72 76191976
    B. Patterson 9/18/71 76199176
    C. Patterson 9/18/72 76199176
    D. Patterson 9/18/71 76919176

10.____

Questions 11-15.

DIRECTIONS: Questions 11 through 15 consist of groups of numbers and letters which you are to compare. For each question, you are to choose the option (A, B, C, or D) in Column I which EXACTLY matches the group of numbers and letters given in Column I.

SAMPLE QUESTION

Column I
B92466

Column II
A. B92644
B. B94266
C. A92466
D. B92466

The correct answer is D. Only Option D in Column II shows the group of numbers and letters EXACTLY as it appears in Column I. Now answer Questions 11 through 15 in the same manner.

	Column I		Column II	
11.	925AC5	A.	952CA5	11.____
		B.	925AC5	
		C.	952AC5	
		D.	925CA6	
12.	Y006925	A.	Y060925	12.____
		B.	Y006295	
		C.	Y006529	
		D.	Y006925	
13.	J236956	A.	J236956	13.____
		B.	J326965	
		C.	J239656	
		D.	J932656	
14.	AB6952	A.	AB6952	14.____
		B.	AB9625	
		C.	AB9652	
		D.	AB6925	
15.	X259361	A.	X529361	15.____
		B.	X259631	
		C.	X523961	
		D.	X259361	

Questions 16-25.

DIRECTIONS: Each of questions 16 through 25 consists of three lines of code letters and three lines of numbers. The numbers on each line should correspond with the code letters on the same line in accordance with the table below.

Code Letter	S	V	W	A	Q	M	X	E	G	K
Corresponding Number	0	1	2	3	4	5	5	7	8	9

On some of the lines, an error exists in the coding. Compare the letters and numbers in each question carefully. If you find an error or errors on:
    only one of the lines in the question, mark your answer A;
    any two lines in the question, mark your answer B;
    all three lines in the question, mark your answer C;
    none of the lines in the question, mark your answer D.

SAMPLE QUESTION

WQGKSXG	2489068
XEKVQMA	6591453
KMAESXV	9527061

In the above sample, the first line is correct since each code letter listed has the correct corresponding number. On the second line, an error exists because code letter E should have the number 7 instead of the number 5. On the third line, an error exists because the code letter A should have the number 3 instead of the number 2. Since there are errors in two of the three lines, the correct answer is B. Now answer Questions 16 through 25 in the same manner.

16. SWQEKGA   0247983   16.____
    KEAVSXM   9731065
    SSAXGKQ   0036894

17. QAMKMVS   4259510   17.____
    MGGEASX   5897306
    KSWMKWS   9125920

18. WKXQWVE   2964217   18.____
    QKXXQVA   4966413
    AWMXGVS   3253810

19. GMMKASE   8559307   19.____
    AWVSKSW   3210902
    QAVSVGK   4310189

20. XGKQSMK   6894049   20.____
    QSVKEAS   4019730
    GSMXKMV   8057951

21. AEKMWSG   3195208   21.____
    MKQSVQK   5940149
    XGQAEVW   6843712

22. XGMKAVS   6858310   22.____
    SKMAWEQ   0953174
    GVMEQSA   8167403

23. VQSKAVE   1489317   23.____
    WQGKAEM   2489375
    MEGKAWQ   5689324

24. XMQVSKG   6541098   24.____
    QMEKEWS   4579720
    KMEVGKG   9571983

25. GKVAMEW   88912572   25.____
     AXMVKAE   3651937
     KWAGMAV   9238531

Questions 26-35.

DIRECTIONS: Each of Questions 26 through 35 consists of a column of figures. For each question, add the column of figures and choose the correct answer from the four choices given.

26. 5,665.43   26.____
     2,356.69
     6,447.24
     7,239.65

     A. 20,698.01   B. 21,709.01
     C. 21,718.01   D. 22,609.01

27. 817,209.55   27.____
     264,354.29
      82,368.76
     849,964.89

     A. 1,893.977.49   B. 1,989,988.39
     C. 2,009,077.39   D. 2,013,897.49

28. 156,366.89   28.____
     249,973.23
     823,229.49
      56,869.45

     A. 1,286,439.06   B. 1,287,521.06
     C. 1,297,539.06   D. 1,296,421.06

29.   23,422.15   29.____
     149,696.24
     238,377.53
      86,289.79
     505,533.63

     A. 989,229.34   B. 999,879.34
     C. 1,003,330.34   D. 1,023,329.34

30. 2,468,926.70 30.____
    656,842.28
    49,723.15
    832,369.59

    A. 3,218,062.72　　　　　　　B. 3,808,092.72
    C. 4,007,861.72　　　　　　　D. 4,818,192.72

31.   524,201.52 31.____
    7,775,678.51
    8,345,299.63
    40,628,898.08
    31,374,670.07

    A. 88,646,647.81　　　　　　B. 88,646,747.91
    C. 88,648,647.91　　　　　　D. 88,648,747.81

32. 6,824,829.40 32.____
    682,482.94
    5,542,015.27
    775,678.51
    7,732,507.25

    A. 21,557,513.37　　　　　　B. 21,567,513.37
    C. 22,567,503.37　　　　　　D. 22,567,513.37

33. 22,109,405.58 33.____
    6,097,093.43
    5,050,073.99
    8,118,050.05
    4,313,980.82

    A. 45,688,593.87　　　　　　B. 45,688,603.87
    C. 45,689,593.87　　　　　　D. 45,689,603.87

34. 79,324,114.19 34.____
    99,848,129.74
    43,331,653.31
    41,610,207.14

    A. 264,114,104.38　　　　　　B. 264,114,114.38
    C. 265,114,114.38　　　　　　D. 265,214,104.38

35. 33,729,653.94
    5,959,342.58
    26,052,715.47
    4,452,669.52
    7,079,953.59

35.____

A. 76,374,334.10
B. 76,375,334.10
C. 77,274,335.10
D. 77,275,335.10

Questions 36-40.

DIRECTIONS: Each of Questions 36 through 40 consists of a single number in Column I and four options in Column II. For each question, you are to choose the option (A, B, C, or D) in Column II which EXACTLY matches the number in Column I.

SAMPLE QUESTION

Column I
5965121

Column II
A. 5956121
B. 5965121
C. 5966121
D. 5965211

The correct answer is B. Only Option B shows the number EXACTLY as it appears in Column I. Now answer Questions 36 through 40 in the same manner.

	Column I	Column II	
36.	9643242	A. 9643242 B. 9462342 C. 9642442 D. 9463242	36.____
37.	3572477	A. 3752477 B. 3725477 C. 3572477 D. 3574277	37.____
38.	5276101	A. 5267101 B. 5726011 C. 5271601 D. 5276101	38.____
39.	4469329	A. 4496329 B. 4469329 C. 4496239 D. 4469239	39.____

40. 2326308   A. 2236308   40._____
                      B. 2233608
                      C. 2326308
                      D. 2323608

KEY (CORRECT ANSWERS)

1.	D	11.	B	21.	A	31.	D
2.	A	12.	D	22.	C	32.	A
3.	B	13.	A	23.	B	33.	B
4.	D	14.	A	24.	D	34.	A
5.	B	15.	D	25.	A	35.	C
6.	C	16.	D	26.	B	36.	A
7.	A	17.	C	27.	D	37.	C
8.	C	18.	A	28.	A	38.	D
9.	A	19.	D	29.	C	39.	B
10.	B	20.	B	30.	C	40.	C

TEST 2

DIRECTIONS: Each question or incomplete statement is followed by several suggested answers or completions. Select the one that BEST answers the question or completes the statement. *PRINT THE LETTER OF THE CORRECT ANSWER IN THE SPACE AT THE RIGHT.*

Questions 1-5.

DIRECTIONS: Each of Questions 1 through 5 consists of a name and a dollar amount. In each question, the name and dollar amount in Column II should be an EXACT copy of the name and dollar amount in Column I. If there is:
- a mistake only in the name, mark your answer A;
- a mistake only in the dollar amount, mark your answer B;
- a mistake in both the name and the dollar amount, mark your answer C;
- no mistake in either the name or the dollar amount, mark your answer D.

SAMPLE QUESTION

Column I	Column II
George Peterson	George Petersson
$125.50	$125.50

Compare the name and dollar amount in Column II with the name and dollar amount in Column I. The name *Petersson* in Column II is spelled *Peterson* in Column I. The amount is the same in both columns. Since there is a mistake only in the name, the answer to the sample question is A. Now answer Questions 1 through 5 in the same manner.

	Column I	Column II	
1.	Susanne Shultz $3440	Susanne Schultz $3440	1.____
2.	Anibal P. Contrucci $2121.61	Anibel P. Contrucci $2112.61	2.____
3.	Eugenio Mendoza $12.45	Eugenio Mendozza $12.45	3.____
4.	Maurice Gluckstadt $4297	Maurice Gluckstadt $4297	4.____
5.	John Pampellonne $4656.94	John Pammpellonne $4566.94	5.____

Questions 6-11.

DIRECTIONS: Each of Questions 6 through 11 consist of a set of names and addresses, which you are to compare. In each question, the name and addresses in Column II should be an EXACT copy of the name and address in Column I. If there is:
- a mistake only in the name, mark your answer A;
- a mistake only in the address, mark your answer B;
- a mistake in both the name and address, mark your answer C;
- no mistake in either the name or address, mark your answer D.

SAMPLE QUESTION

Column I	Column II
Michael Filbert	Michael Filbert
456 Reade Street	645 Reade Street
New York, N.Y. 10013	New York, N.Y. 10013

Since there is a mistake only in the address (the street number should be 456 instead of 645), the answer to the sample question is B. Now answer Questions 6 through 11 in the same manner.

	Column I	Column II	
6.	Hilda Goettelmann 55 Lenox Rd. Brooklyn, N.Y. 11226	Hilda Goettelman 55 Lenox Ave. Brooklyn, N.Y. 11226	6.____
7.	Arthur Sherman 2522 Batchelder St. Brooklyn, N.Y. 11235	Arthur Sharman 2522 Batcheder St. Brooklyn, N.Y. 11253	7.____
8.	Ralph Barnett 300 West 28 Street New York, New York 10001	Ralph Barnett 300 West 28 Street New York, New York 10001	8.____
9.	George Goodwin 135 Palmer Avenue Staten Island, New York 10302	George Godwin 135 Palmer Avenue Staten Island, New York 10302	9.____
10.	Alonso Ramirez 232 West 79 Street New York, N.Y. 10024	Alonso Ramirez 223 West 79 Street New York, N.Y. 10024	10.____
11.	Cynthia Graham 149-34 83 Street Howard Beach, N.Y. 11414	Cynthia Graham 149-35 83 Street Howard Beach, N.Y. 11414	11.____

Questions 12-20.

DIRECTIONS: Questions 12 through 20 are problems in subtraction. For each question do the subtraction and select your answer from the four choices given.

12. 232,921.85
    -179,587.68

    A. 52,433.17   B. 52,434.17
    C. 53,334.17   D. 53,343,17

    12.____

13. 5,531,876.29
    -3,897,158.36

    A. 1,634,717.93   B. 1,644,718.93
    C. 1,734,717.93   D. 1,7234,718.93

    13.____

14. 1,482,658.22
    -937,925.76

    A. 544,633.46   B. 544,732.46
    C. 545,632.46   D. 545,732.46

    14.____

15. 937,828.17
    -259,673.88

    A. 678,154.29   B. 679,154.29
    C. 688,155.39   D. 699,155.39

    15.____

16. 760,412.38
    -263,465.95

    A. 496,046.43   B. 496,946.43
    C. 496,956.43   D. 497,046.43

    16.____

17. 3,203,902.26
    -2,933,087.96

    A. 260,814.30   B. 269,824.30
    C. 270,814.30   D. 270,824.30

    17.____

18. 1,023,468.71
    -934,678.88

    A. 88,780.83   B. 88,789.83
    C. 88,880.83   D. 88,889.83

    18.____

4 (#2)

19. 831,549.47
    -772,814.78

    A. 58,734.69   B. 58,834.69
    C. 59,735.69   D. 59,834.69

19.____

20. 6,306,181.74
    -3,617,376.99

    A. 2,687,904.99   B. 2,688,904.99
    C. 2,689,804.99   D. 2,799,905.99

20.____

Questions 21-30.

DIRECTIONS: Each of Questions 21 through 30 consists of three lines of code letters and three lines of numbers. The numbers on each line should correspond with the code letters on the same line in accordance with the table below.

Code Letter	J	U	B	T	Y	D	K	R	L	P
Corresponding Number	0	1	2	3	4	5	5	7	8	9

On some of the lines, an error exists in the coding. Compare the letters and numbers in each question carefully. If you find an error or errors on:
    only *one* of the lines in the question, mark your answer A;
    any *two* lines in the question, mark your answer B;
    all *three* lines in the question, mark your answer C;
    none of the lines in the question, mark your answer D.

SAMPLE QUESTION

    BJRPYUR   2079417
    DTBPYKJ   5328460
    YKLDBLT   4685283

In the above sample, the first line is correct since each code letter listed has the correct corresponding number. On the second line, an error exists because code letter P should have the number 9 instead of the number 8. The third line is correct since each code letter listed has the correct corresponding number. Since there is an error in *one* of the three lines, the correct answer is A. Now answer Questions 21 through 30 in the same manner.

21.   BYPDTJL   2495308
     PLRDTJU   9815301
     DTJRYLK   5207486

21.____

22.   RPBYRJK   7934706
     PKTYLBU   9624821
     KDLPJYR   6489047

22.____

23.	TPYBUJR	3942107	23.____
	BYRKPTU	2476931	
	DUKPYDL	5169458	
24.	KBYDLPL	6345898	24.____
	BLRKBRU	2876261	
	JTULDYB	0318542	
25.	LDPYDKR	8594567	25.____
	BDKDRJL	2565708	
	BDRPLUJ	2679810	
26.	PLRLBPU	9858291	26.____
	LPYKRDJ	88936750	
	TDKPDTR	3569527	
27.	RKURPBY	7617924	27.____
	RYUKPTJ	7426930	
	RTKPTJD	7369305	
28.	DYKPBJT	5469203	28.____
	KLPJBTL	6890238	
	TKPLBJP	3698209	
29.	BTPRJYL	2397148	29.____
	LDKUTYR	8561347	
	YDBLRPJ	4528190	
30.	ULPBKYT	1892643	30.____
	KPDTRBJ	6953720	
	YLKJPTB	4860932	

KEY (CORRECT ANSWERS)

1.	A	11.	D	21.	B
2.	C	12.	C	22.	C
3.	A	13.	A	23.	D
4.	D	14.	B	24.	B
5.	C	15.	A	25.	A
6.	C	16.	B	26.	C
7.	C	17.	C	27.	A
8.	D	18.	B	28.	D
9.	A	19.	A	29.	B
10.	B	20.	B	30.	D

NAME AND NUMBER COMPARISONS

COMMENTARY

This test seeks to measure your ability and disposition to do a job carefully and accurately, your attention to exactness and preciseness of detail, your alertness and versatility in discerning similarities and differences between things, and your power in systematically handling written language symbols.

It is actually a test of your ability to do academic and/or clerical work, using the basic elements of verbal (qualitative) and mathematical (quantitative) learning—words and numbers.

EXAMINATION SECTION

TEST 1

DIRECTIONS: In each line across the page there are three names or numbers that are much alike. Compare the three names or numbers and decide which ones are exactly alike. *PRINT IN THE SPACE AT THE RIGHT THE LETTER:*
  A. if all THREE names or numbers are exactly alike
  B. if only the FIRST and SECOND names or numbers are ALIKE
  C. if only the FIRST and THIRD names or numbers are alike
  D. if only the SECOND or THIRD names or numbers are alike
  E. if ALL THREE names or numbers are DIFFERENT

1.	Davis Hazen	David Hozen	David Hazen	1.____
2.	Lois Appel	Lois Appel	Lois Apfel	2.____
3.	June Allan	Jane Allan	Jane Allan	3.____
4.	10235	10235	10235	4.____
5.	32614	32164	32614	5.____

TEST 2

1.	2395890	2395890	2395890	1.____
2.	1926341	1926347	1926314	2.____
3.	E. Owens McVey	E. Owen McVey	E. Owen McVay	3.____
4.	Emily Neal Rouse	Emily Neal Rowse	Emily Neal Rowse	4.____
5.	H. Merritt Audubon	H. Merriott Audubon	H. Merritt Audubon	5.____

TEST 3

1. 6219354	6219354	6219354	1.____
2. 231793	2312793	2312793	2.____
3. 1065407	1065407	1065047	3.____
4. Francis Ransdell	Frances Ramsdell	Francis Ramsdell	4.____
5. Cornelius Detwiler	Cornelius Detwiler	Cornelius Detwiler	5.____

TEST 4

1. 6452054	6452564	6542054	1.____
2. 8501268	8501268	8501286	2.____
3. Ella Burk Newham	Ella Burk Newnham	Elena Burk Newnham	3.____
4. Jno. K. Ravencroft	Jno. H. Ravencroft	Jno. H. Ravencoft	4.____
5. Martin Wills Pullen	Martin Wills Pulen	Martin Wills Pullen	5.____

TEST 5

1. 3457988	3457986	3457986	1.____
2. 4695682	4695862	4695682	2.____
3. Stricklund Kaneydy	Sticklund Kanedy	Stricklund Kanedy	3.____
4. Joy Harlor Witner	Joy Harloe Witner	Joy Harloe Witner	4.____
5. R.M.O. Uberroth	R.M.O. Uberroth	R.N.O. Uberroth	5.____

TEST 6

1.	1592514	1592574	1592574	1.____
2.	2010202	2010202	2010220	2.____
3.	6177396	6177936	6177396	3.____
4.	Drusilla S. Ridgeley	Drusilla S. Ridgeley	Drusilla S. Ridgeley	4.____
5.	Andrei I. Tooumantzev	Andrei I. Tourmantzev	Andrei I. Toumantzov	5.____

TEST 7

1.	5261383	5261383	5261338	1.____
2.	8125690	8126690	8125609	2.____
3.	W.E. Johnston	W.E. Johnson	W.E. Johnson	3.____
4.	Vergil L. Muller	Vergil L. Muller	Vergil L. Muller	4.____
5.	Atherton R. Warde	Asheton R. Warde	Atherton P. Warde	5.____

TEST 8

1.	013469.5	023469.5	02346.95	1.____
2.	33376	333766	333766	2.____
3.	Ling-Temco-Vought	Ling-Tenco-Vought	Ling-Temco Vought	3.____
4.	Lorilard Corp.	Lorillard Corp.	Lorrilard Corp.	4.____
5.	American Agronomics Corporation	American Agronomics Corporation	American Agronomic Corporation	5.____

TEST 9

1.	436592864	436592864	436592864	1.____
2.	197765123	197755123	197755123	2.____
3.	Dewaay Cortvriendt International S.A.	Deway Cortvriendt International S.A.	Deway Corturiendt International S.A.	3.____
4.	Crèdit Lyonnais	Crèdit Lyonnais	Crèdit Lyonais	4.____
5.	Algemene Bank Nederland N.V.	Algamene Bank Nederland N.V.	Algemene Bank Naderland N.V.	5.____

TEST 10

1.	00032572	0.0032572	00032522	1.____
2.	399745	399745	398745	2.____
3.	Banca Privata Finanziaria S.p.A.	Banca Privata Finanzaria S.P.A.	Banca Privata Finanziaria S.P.A.	3.____
4.	Eastman Dillon, Union Securities & Co.	Eastman Dillon, Union Securities Co.	Eastman Dillon, Union Securities & Co.	4.____
5.	Arnhold and S. Bleichroeder, Inc.	Arnhold & S. Bleichroeder, Inc.	Arnold and S. Bleichroeder, Inc.	5.____

TEST 11

DIRECTIONS: Answer the questions below on the basis of the following instructions: For each such numbered set of names, addresses, and numbers listed in Columns I and II, select your answer from the following options:
A. The names in Columns I and II are different
B. The addresses in Columns I and II are different
C. The numbers in Columns I and II are different
D. The names, addresses and numbers are identical

1. Francis Jones
   62 Stately Avenue
   96-12446

   Francis Jones
   62 Stately Avenue
   96-21446

   1._____

2. Julio Montez
   19 Ponderosa Road
   56-73161

   Julio Montez
   19 Ponderosa Road
   56-71361

   2._____

3. Mary Mitchell
   2314 Melbourne Drive
   68-92172

   Mary Mitchell
   2314 Melbourne Drive
   68-92172

   3._____

4. Harry Patterson
   25 Dunne Street
   14-33430

   Harry Patterson
   25 Dunne Street
   14-34330

   4._____

5. Patrick Murphy
   171 West Hosmer Street
   93-81214

   Patrick Murphy
   171 West Hosmer Street
   93-18214

   5._____

TEST 12

1. August Schultz
816 St. Clair Avenue
53-40149

August Schultz
816 St. Claire Avenue
53-40149

1.____

2. George Taft
72 Runnymede Street
47-04033

George Taft
72 Runnymede Street
47-04023

2.____

3. Angus Henderson
1418 Madison Street
81-76375

Angus Henderson
1418 Madison Street
81-76375

3.____

4. Carolyn Mazur
12 Rivenlew Road
38-99615

Carolyn Mazur
12 Rivervane Road
38-99615

4.____

5. Adele Russell
1725 Lansing Lane
72-91962

Adela Russell
1725 Lansing Lane
72-91962

5.____

TEST 13

DIRECTIONS: The following questions are based on the instructions given below. In each of the following questions, the 3-line name and address in Column I is the master-list entry, and the 3-line entry in Column II is the information to be checked against the master list.
If there is one line that is NOT exactly alike, mark your answer A.
If there are two lines NOT exactly alike, mark your answer B.
If there are three lines NOT exactly alike, mark your answer C.
If the lines ALL are exactly alike, mark your answer D.

1. Jerome A. Jackson   Jerome A. Johnson   1.____
    1243 14th Avenue   1234 14th Avenue
    New York, N.Y. 10023   New York, N.Y. 10023

2. Sophie Strachtheim   Sophie Strachtheim   2.____
    33-28 Connecticut Ave.   33-28 Connecticut Ave.
    Far Rockaway, N.Y. 11697   Far Rockaway, N.Y. 11697

3. Elisabeth NT. Gorrell   Elizabeth NT. Correll   3.____
    256 Exchange St   256 Exchange St.
    New York, N.Y. 10013   New York, N.Y. 10013

4. Maria J. Gonzalez   Maria J. Gonzalez   4.____
    7516 E. Sheepshead Rd.   7516 N. Shepshead Rd.
    Brooklyn, N.Y. 11240   Brooklyn, N.Y. 11240

5. Leslie B. Brautenweiler   Leslie B. Brautenwieler   5.____
    21-57A Seller Terr.   21-75ASeiler Terr.
    Flushing, N.Y. 11367   Flushing, N.J. 11367

KEY (CORRECT ANSWERS)

TEST 1	TEST 2	TEST 3	TEST 4	TEST 5	TEST 6	TEST 7
1. E	1. A	1. A	1. E	1. D	1. D	1. B
2. B	2. E	2. A	2. B	2. C	2. B	2. E
3. D	3. E	3. B	3. E	3. E	3. C	3. D
4. A	4. D	4. E	4. E	4. D	4. A	4. A
5. C	5. C	5. A	5. C	5. B	5. E	5. E

TEST 8	TEST 9	TEST 10	TEST 11	TEST 12	TEST 13
1. E	1. A	1. E	1. C	1. B	1. B
2. D	2. D	2. B	2. C	2. C	2. D
3. E	3. E	3. E	3. D	3. D	3. A
4. E	4. E	4. C	4. C	4. B	4. A
5. B	5. E	5. E	5. C	5. A	5. C

ARITHMETICAL REASONING

EXAMINATION SECTION

TEST 1

DIRECTIONS: Each question or incomplete statement is followed by several suggested answers or completions. Select the one that BEST answers the question or completes the statement. *PRINT THE LETTER OF THE CORRECT ANSWER IN THE SPACE AT THE RIGHT.*

1. Assume that it takes approximately 1 1/2 minutes to unload a dozen identical items from a delivery truck.
   At this speed, the amount of time it should take to unload a shipment of 876 items is, MOST NEARLY, _____ minutes.
   A. 90   B. 100   C. 110   D. 120

   1._____

2. Assume that a shop clerk has received a bill of $108 for a delivery of clamps which cost $4.32 per dozen.
   How many clamps should there be in this delivery?
   A. 25   B. 36   C. 300   D. 360

   2._____

3. Employee A has not used any leave time and has accumulated a total of 45 leave-days.
   How many months did it take employee A to have accumulated 45 leave-days if the accrual rate is 1 2/3 days per months?
   A. 25   B. 27   C. 29   D. 31

   3._____

4. A shop clerk is notified that only 75 bolts can be supplied by Vendor A.
   If this represents 12.5% of the total requisition, then how many bolts were originally ordered?
   A. 125   B. 600   C. 700   D. 900

   4._____

5. An enclosed square-shaped storage area with sides of 16 feet each has a safe-load capacity of 250 pounds per square foot.
   The MAXIMUM evenly distributed weight that can be stored in this area is _____ lbs.
   A. 1,056   B. 4,000   C. 64,000   D. 102,400

   5._____

6. A clerical employee completed 70 progress reports the first week, 87 the second week, and 80 the third week.
   Assuming a 4-week month, how many progress reports must the clerk complete in the fourth week in order to attain an average of 85 progress reports per week for the month?
   A. 93   B. 103   C. 113   D. 133

   6._____

2 (#1)

7. On the first of the month, Shop X received a delivery of 150 gallons of lubricating oil. During the month, the following amounts of oil were used on lubricating work each week: 30 quarts, 36 quarts, 20 quarts, and 48 quarts.
The amount of lubricating oil remaining at the end of the month was _____ gallons.

    A. 4   B. 33.5   C. 41.5   D. 116.5

7.____

8. For working a 35-hour week, Employee A earns a gross amount of $160.30. For each hour that Employee A works over 40 hours a week, he is entitled to 1 1/2 times his hourly wage rate.
If Employee A worked 9 hours on Monday, 8 hours on Tuesday, 9 hours 30 minutes on Wednesday, 9 hours 15 minutes on Thursday, and 9 hours 15 minutes on Friday, what should his gross salary be for that week?

    A. $206.10   B. $210.68   C. $217.55   D. $229.00

8.____

9. An enclosed cube-shaped storage bay has dimensions of 12 feet by 12 feet by 12 feet. Standard procedure requires that there be at least 1 foot of space between the walls, the ceiling and the stored items.
What is the MAXIMUM number of cube-shaped boxes with length, width, and height of 1 foot each that can be stored on 1-foot high pallets in this bay?

    A. 1,000   B. 1,331   C. 1,452   D. 1,728

9.____

10. Assume that two ceilings are to be painted. One ceiling measures 30 feet by 15 feet and the second 45 feet by 60 feet.
If one quart of paint will cover 60 square feet of ceiling, approximately how much paint will be required to paint the two ceilings?

    A. 6 gallons   B. 10 gallons   C. 13 gallons   D. 18 gallons

10.____

KEY (CORRECT ANSWERS)

1.	C	6.	B
2.	C	7.	D
3.	B	8.	C
4.	B	9.	A
5.	C	10.	C

SOLUTIONS TO PROBLEMS

1. 876 ÷ 12 = 73. Then, (73)(1 1/2) = 109.5 ≈ 110 minutes.

2. $108 ÷ $4.32 = 25. Then, (25)(12) = 300 clamps.

3. 45 ÷ 1 1/2 = 27 months

4. 75 ÷ .125 = 600 bolts

5. (16)(16)(250) == 64,000 pounds

6. (85)(4) = 340. Then, 340 – 70 – 87 – 80 = 103 progress reports.

7. Changing every calculation to gallons, the amount of oil remaining is 150 – 7.5 – 9 – 5 – 12 = 116.5.

8. 9 + 8 + 9.5 + 9.25 + 9.25 = 45 hours. His gross pay will be ($4.58)(40) + ($6.87)(5) = $217.55. (Note: To get his regular hourly wages, divide $160.30 by 35.)

9. 12 – 1 – 1 =10. Maximum number of boxes is $(10)^3$ = 1000.

10. First ceiling contains (30)(15) = 450 sq.ft., whereas the second ceiling contains (45)(60) = 2700 sq.ft. The total sq.ft. = 3150. Now, 3150 ÷ 60 = 52.5 quarts of paint = 13.125 or 13 gallons.

TEST 2

DIRECTIONS: Each question or incomplete statement is followed by several suggested answers or completions. Select the one that BEST answers the question or completes the statement. *PRINT THE LETTER OF THE CORRECT ANSWER IN THE SPACE AT THE RIGHT.*

1. A piping sketch is drawn to a scale of 1/8" = 1 foot.
   A vertical steam line measuring 3/4" on the sketch would have an actual length of _____ feet.
   A. 16   B. 22   C. 24   D. 28

2. Three lengths of pipe 1'10", 3'2 1/2", and 5'7 1/2", respectively, are to be cut from a pipe 14'0" long.
   Allowing 1/8" for each pipe cut, the length of pipe remaining is
   A. 3'1 1/8"   B. 3'2 1/2"   C. 3'3 1/2"   D. 3'3 5/8"

3. Assume that a steamfitter's helper earns $11.16 an hour and that he works 250 seven-hour days a year.
   His gross yearly salary will be
   A. 19,430   B. $19,530   C. $19,650   D. $19,780

4. A pipe having an inside diameter of 3.48 inches and a wall thickness of .18 inches, will have an outside diameter of _____ inches.
   A. 3.84   B. 3.64   C. 3.57   D. 3.51

5. A rectangular steel bar having a volume of 30 cubic inches, a width of 2 inches, and a height of 3 inches will have a length of _____ inches.
   A. 12   B. 10   C. 8   D. 5

6. A pipe weighs 20.4 pounds per foot of length.
   The total weight of eight pieces of this pipe with each piece 20 feet in length is MOST NEARLY _____ pounds.
   A. 460   B. 1680   C. 2420   D. 3260

7. In last year's budget, $7,500 was spent for office supplies. Of this amount, 60% was spent for paper supplies.
   If the price of paper has risen 20% over last year's price, then the amount that will be spent this year on paper supplies, assuming the same quantity will be purchased, will be
   A. $3,600   B. $5,200   C. $5,400   D. $6,000

8. If it takes 4 painters 54 days to do a certain paint job, then the time it should take 5 painters working at the same speed to do the same job is MOST NEARLY _____ days.
   A. 3 1/2   B. 4   C. 4 1/2   D. 5

9. A foreman assigns a gang foreman to supervise a job which must be completed at the end of 7 working days. The gang foreman has 8 maintainers in his gang. At the end of 3 working days, although the work has been efficiently done, the job is only one-third completed.
In order to complete the job on time, without overtime, the gang foreman should request that he be given _____ more maintainers.
   A. 3   B. 4   C. 5   D. 6

9._____

10. One shipment of 70 shovels costs $140. A second shipment of 130 shovels costs $208.00.
The average cost per shovel for both shipments is MOST NEARLY
   A. $1.60   B. $1.75   C. $2.00   D. $2.50

10._____

KEY (CORRECT ANSWERS)

1.	D	6.	D
2.	D	7.	C
3.	B	8.	C
4.	A	9.	B
5.	D	10.	B

SOLUTIONS TO PROBLEMS

1. 3 1/2 ÷ 1/8 = 28 feet.

2. 14' − 1'10" − 3' 1/2" − 5'7 1/2" − 1/8" − 1/8" − 1/8" = 3'3 5/8"

3. (250(7) = 1750 hours. Then, ($11.16)(1750) = $19,530

4. Outside diameter = 3.48 + .18 + .18 = 3.84 inches

5. Length is 30 ÷ 2 ÷ 3 = 5 inches

6. (20)(8) = 160 feet. Then, (160)(20.4) = 3264 ≈ 3260 pounds

7. ($7,500)(.60) = $4,500. Then, ($4,500)(1.20) = $5,400

8. Let x = required days. Since this is an inverse ratio, 4/5 = x/5 1/2. Then, 5x = 22. Solving, x = 4.4 ≈ 4 1/2

9. (8)(3) = 24 man-days were needed to complete 1/3 of the job.
   Since 2/3 of the job remains, the foreman will need 48 man-days for the remaining 4 days. This requires 12 men. Since he has 8 currently, he will need 4 more workers.

10. Average cost per shovel is ($140 + $208) ÷ (70+130) = $1.74, which is closest to $1.75.

TEST 3

DIRECTIONS: Each question or incomplete statement is followed by several suggested answers or completions. Select the one that BEST answers the question or completes the statement. *PRINT THE LETTER OF THE CORRECT ANSWER IN THE SPACE AT THE RIGHT.*

1. Assume that your warehouse received a shipment of 600 articles. A sample of 60 articles was inspected. Of this sample, one article was wholly defective and four articles were partly defective.
   On the basis of this sampling, you would expect the total number of defective articles in this shipment to be
   A. 5   B. 10   C. 40   D. 50

   1.____

2. Assume that you have been instructed to order mineral spirits as soon as the supply-on-hand falls to the level required for sixty days of issue.
   If the total amount of mineral spirits on hand is 960 gallons and you issue an average of 8 gallons of mineral spirits per day, and your warehouse works a five-day week, you will be required to order mineral spirits in _____ working days.
   A. 50   B. 60   C. 70   D. 80

   2.____

3. Assume that you work in a one-story warehouse where the total available floor space measures 175 feet by 140 feet. Of this floor space, one area measuring 35 feet by 75 feet is used for storing materials handling equipment, another area is measuring 10 feet by 21 feet is used for office space, and the remaining floor space is available for storage.
   The amount of floor space available for storage in this one-story warehouse is _____ square feet.
   A. 21,665   B. 21,875   C. 24,290   D. $24,500

   3.____

4. Assume that linoleum tiles measuring 9 inches by 9 inches are packed ten to a box and each box costs $3.50.
   The cost of buying enough linoleum tiles to cover an area measuring 15 feet by 21 feet is
   A. $98.00   B. $110.25   C. $196.00   D. $220.50

   4.____

5. The number of boxes measuring 3 inches by 3 inches by 3 inches that will fit into a carton measuring 2 feet by 4 feet is
   A. 2,048   B. 2,645   C. 7,936   D. 23,808

   5.____

6. The stock inventory card for paint, white, flat, one-gallon, has the following entries:

Date	Received	Shipped	Balance
April 12	-	25	75
April 13	50	75	
April 14	-	10	
April 15	25		
April 16			

   6.____

2 (#3)

The balance on hand at the close of business on April 15 should be
   A. 40   B. 45   C. 55   D. 65

7. The cost of one dozen pieces of screening, each measuring 4 feet 6 inches at $.10 per square foot is
   A. $22.50   B. $25.00   C. $27.00   D. $27.60

8. Assume that it takes an average of ten man-hours to stack four tons of a particular item.
   In order to stack 80 tons, the number of men required to complete the job in twenty hours is
   A. 10   B. 20   C. 30   D. 40

9. Assume that you are required to relocate 5,000 reams of unboxed paper using only manual labor. The average time required for one laborer to pick 12 reams, carry them to the new location, and store them properly is ten minutes.
   In order to complete this relocation task within one working day of seven hours, the MINIMUM number of laborers you should assign to this task is
   A. 10   B. 15   C. 24   D. 70

10. Assume that you receive a shipment of 9 boxes of paper towels. Each box contains 6 dozen packages. Each package contains 200 paper towels. The total cost of the shipment of boxes is $64.80. The unit of issue for paper towels is the package.
    The unit cost of the paper towels is
    A. $.10   B. $.90   C. $1.20   D. $7.20

KEY (CORRECT ANSWERS)

1. D   6. D
2. B   7. C
3. A   8. A
4. C   9. A
5. A   10. A

3 (#3)

SOLUTIONS TO PROBLEMS

1. Solve for x: 5/60 = x/600. Then, x = 50

2. 960 ÷ 8 = 120 days. Then, 120 – 60 = 60 days

3. Storage area is (175)(140) – (35)(75) – (10)(21) = 21,665 sq.ft.

4. 9 × 9 = 81 sq.in. (81)(10) = 810 sq.in. of tiles cost $3.50. (15ft)(21ft) = (180)(252) = 45,360 sq.in. Now, 45,360 ÷ 810 = 56 boxes. Finally, (56)($3.50) = $196

5. (2ft)(4ft)(4ft) = (24 in)(48 in)(48 in) = 55,296 sq.in. Then, 55,296/27 = 2048 boxes.

6. Balance at end of April 13th is 75 + 50 – 75 = 50
   Balance at end of April 14th is 50 + 0 – 10 = 40
   Balance at end of April 15th is 40 + 25 – 0 = 65

7. (4 1/2)(5) = 224 sq.ft. Then, (22)($0.10) = $2.25 per piece. The cost of 12 pieces is ($2.25)(12) = $27

8. If 10 man-hours are needed for 4 tons, then 200 man-hours are needed for 80 tons. The number of men needed to do the job in 20 hours is 200 ÷ 20 = 10

9. 7 hours = 420 minutes and 420 ÷ 10 = 42.
   Then, (42)(12) = 504 reams transported per day for each laborer. Now, 5000 ÷ 504 ≈ 9.92, which gets rounded up to 10.

10. (9)(72) = 648 package. Then, $64.80 ÷ 648 = $0.10

DOCUMENTS AND FORMS
PREPARING WRITTEN MATERIALS
EXAMINATION SECTION
TEST 1

DIRECTIONS: Each question or incomplete statement is followed by several suggested answers or completions. Select the one that BEST answers the question or completes the statement. *PRINT THE LETTER OF THE CORRECT ANSWER IN THE SPACE AT THE RIGHT.*

1. Of the following types of documents, it is MOST important to retain and file 1.____
   A. working drafts of reports that have been submitted in final form
   B. copies of letters of good will which conveyed a message that could not be handled by phone
   C. interoffice orders for materials which have been received and verified
   D. interoffice memoranda regarding the routine of standard forms

2. The MAXIMUM number of 2¾" x 4¼" size forms which may be obtained from one ream of 17" x 22" paper is 2.____
   A. 4,000   B. 8,000   C. 12,000   D. 16,000

3. On a general organization chart, staff positions NORMALLY should be pictured 3.____
   A. directly above the line positions to which they report
   B. to the sides of the main flow lines
   C. within the box of the highest level subordinate positions pictured
   D. directly below the line positions which report to them

4. When an administrator is diagramming an office layout, of the following, his PRIMARY job generally should be to indicate the 4.____
   A. lighting intensities that will be required by each operator
   B. noise level that will be produced by the various equipment employed in the office
   C. direction of the work flow and the distance involved in each transfer
   D. durability of major pieces of office equipment currently in use or to be utilized

5. One common guideline or rule-of-thumb ratio for evaluating the efficiency of files is the number of records requested divided by the number of records filed. Generally, if this ratio is very low, it would point MOST directly to the need for 5.____
   A. improving the indexing and coding systems
   B. improving the charge-out procedures
   C. exploring the need for transferring records from active storage to the archives
   D. exploring the need to encourage employees to keep more records in their private files

6. The GREATEST percentage of money spent on preparing and keeping the usual records in an office generally is expended for which one of the following?
   A. Renting space in which to place the record-keeping equipment
   B. Paying salaries of record-preparing and record-keeping personnel
   C. Depreciation of purchased record-preparation and record-keeping machines
   D. Paper and forms upon which to place the records

7. In a certain office, file folders are constantly being removed from the files for use by administrators. At the same time, new material is coming in to be filed in some of these folders.
   Of the following, the BEST way to avoid delays in filing of the new material and to keep track of the removed folders is to
   A. keep a sheet listing all folders removed from the file, who has them, and a follow-update to check on their return; attach to this list new material received for filing
   B. put an "out" slip in the place of any file folder removed, telling what folder is missing, date removed, and who has it; file new material received at front of files
   C. put a temporary "out" folder in place of the one removed, giving title or subject, date removed, and who has it; put into this temporary folder any new material received
   D. keep a list of all folders removed and who has them; forward any new material received for filing while a folder is out to the person who has it

8. Folders labeled "Miscellaneous" should be used in an alphabetic filing system MAINLY to
   A. provide quick access to recent material
   B. avoid setting up individual folders for infrequent correspondence
   C. provide temporary storage for less important documents
   D. temporarily hold papers which will not fit into already crowded individual folders

9. Out-of-date and seldom-used records should be removed periodically from the files because
   A. overall responsibility for records will be transferred to the person in charge of the central storage files
   B. duplicate copies of every record are not needed
   C. valuable filing space will be regained and the time needed to find a current record will be cut down
   D. worthwhile suggestions on improving the filing system will result whenever this is done

10. Of the following, the BEST reason for discarding certain material from office files would be that the
    A. files are crowded
    B. material in the files is old
    C. material duplicates information obtainable from other sources in the files
    D. material is referred to most often by employees in an adjoining office

11. Of the following, the MAIN factor contributing to the expense of maintaining an office procedure manual would be the
    A. infrequent use of the manual
    B. need to revise it regularly
    C. cost of loose-leaf binders
    D. high cost of printing

11.____

12. The suggestion that memos or directives which circulate among subordinates be initialed by each employee is a
    A. *poor* one, because, with modern copying machines, it would be possible to supply every subordinate with a copy of each message for his personal use
    B. *good* one, because it relieves the supervisor of blame for the action of subordinates who have read and initialed the messages
    C. *poor* one, because initialing the memo or directive is no guarantee that the subordinate has read the material
    D. *good* one, because it can be used as a record by the supervisor to show that his subordinates have received the message and were responsible for reading it

12.____

13. Of the following, the MOST important reason for microfilming office records is to
    A. save storage space needed to keep records
    B. make it easier to get records when needed
    C. speed up the classification of information
    D. shorten the time which records must be kept

13.____

14. Your office filing cabinets have become so overcrowded that it is difficult to use the files.
    Of the following, the MOST desirable step for you to take FIRST to relieve this situation would be to
    A. assign your assistant to spend some time each day reviewing the material in the files and to give you his recommendations as to what material may be discarded
    B. discard all material which has been in the files more than a given number of years
    C. submit a request for additional filing cabinets in your next budget request
    D. transfer enough material to the central storage room of your agency to give you the amount of additional filing space needed

14.____

15. In indexing names of business firms and other organizations, one of the rules to be followed is:
    A. The word "and" is considered an indexing unit
    B. When a firm name includes the full name of a person who is not well known, the person's first name is considered as the first indexing unit
    C. Usually, the units in a firm name are indexed in the order in which they are written
    D. When a firm's name is made up of single letters (such as ABC Corp.), the letters taken together are considered as more than one indexing unit

15.____

16. Assume that your unit processes confidential forms which are submitted by persons seeking financial assistance. An individual comes to your office, gives you his name, and states that he would like to look over a form which he sent in about a week ago because he believes he omitted some important information.
    Of the following, the BEST thing for you to do FIRST is to
    A. locate the proper form
    B. call the individual's home telephone number to verify his identity
    C. ask the individual if he has proof of his identity
    D. call the security office

16.____

17. An employee has been assigned to open her division head's mail and place it on his desk. One day, the employee opens a letter which she then notices is marked "Personal."
    Of the following, the BEST action for her to take is to
    A. write "Personal" on the letter and staple the envelope to the back of the letter
    B. ignore the matter and treat the letter the same way as the others
    C. give it to another division head to hold until her own division head comes into the office
    D. leave the letter in the envelope and write "Sorry-opened by mistake" on the envelope, and initial it

17.____

18. The MOST important reason for having a filing system is to
    A. get papers out of the way
    B. have a record of everything that has happened
    C. retain information to justify your actions
    D. enable rapid retrieval of information

18.____

19. The system of filing which is used MOST frequently is called _____ filing.
    A. alphabetic   B. alphanumeric
    C. geographic   D. numeric

19.____

20. In judging the adequacy of a standard office form, which of the following is LEAST important?
    A. Date of the form   B. Legibility of the form
    C. Size of the form   D. Design of the form

20.____

21. Assume that the letters and reports which are dictated to you fall into a few distinct subject-matter areas.
    The practice of trying to familiarize yourself with the terminology in these areas is
    A. *good*, because you will have a basis for commenting on the dictated material
    B. *good*, because it will be easier to take the dictation at the rate at which it is given
    C. *poor*, because the functions and policies of an office are not of your concern
    D. *poor*, because it will take too much time away from your assigned work

21.____

22. A letter was dictated on June 9 and was ready to be typed on June 12. The letter was typed on June 13, signed on June 14, and mailed on June 14. The date that, ORDINARILY, should have appeared on the letter is June
   A. 9   B. 12   C. 13   D. 14

22.____

23. Of the following, the BEST reason for putting the "key point" at the beginning of a letter is that it
   A. may save time for the reader
   B. is standard practice in writing letters
   C. will more likely to be typed correctly
   D. cannot logically be placed elsewhere

23.____

24. As a supervisor, you have been asked to attend committee meetings and take the minutes.
   The body of such minutes GENERALLY consists of
   A. the date and place of the meeting and the list of persons present
   B. an exact verbatim report of everything that was said by each person who spoke
   C. a clear description of each matter discussed and the action decided on
   D. the agenda of the meeting

24.____

25. When typing a rough draft from a recorded transcription, a stenographer under your supervision reaches a spot on the recording that is virtually inaudible.
   Of the following, the MOST advisable action that you should recommend to her is to
   A. guess what the dictator intended to say based on what he said in the parts that are clear
   B. ask the dictator to listen to his unsatisfactory recording
   C. leave an appropriate amount of space for that portion that is inaudible
   D. stop typing the draft and send a note to the dictator identifying the item that could not be completed

25.____

KEY (CORRECT ANSWERS)

1.	D		11.	B
2.	D		12.	D
3.	B		13.	A
4.	C		14.	A
5.	C		15.	C
6.	B		16.	C
7.	C		17.	D
8.	B		18.	D
9.	C		19.	A
10.	C		20.	A

21. B
22. D
23. A
24. C
25. C

TEST 2

DIRECTIONS: Each question or incomplete statement is followed by several suggested answers or completions. Select the one that BEST answers the question or completes the statement. *PRINT THE LETTER OF THE CORRECT ANSWER IN THE SPACE AT THE RIGHT.*

1. To tell a newly employed clerk to fill a top drawer of a four-drawer cabinet with heavy binders which will be often used and to keep lower drawers only partly filled is
   A. *good*, because a tall person would have to bend unnecessarily if he had to use a lower drawer
   B. *bad*, because the file cabinet may tip over when the top drawer is opened
   C. *good*, because it is the most easily reachable drawer for the average person
   D. *bad*, because a person bending down at another drawer may accidentally bang his head on the bottom of the drawer when he straightens up

2. If you have requisitioned a "ream" of paper in order to duplicate a single page office announcement, how many announcements can be printed from the one package of paper?
   A. 200   B. 500   C. 700   D. 1,000

3. In the operations of a government agency, a voucher is ORDINARILY used to
   A. refer someone to the agency for a position or assignment
   B. certify that an agency's records of financial transactions are accurate
   C. order payment from agency funds of a stated amount to an individual
   D. enter a statement of official opinion in the records of the agency

4. Of the following types of cards used in filing systems, the one which is generally MOST helpful in locating records which might be filed under more than one subject is the _____ card.
   A. out
   B. tickler
   C. cross-reference
   D. visible index

5. The type of filing system in which one does NOT need to refer to a card index in order to find the folder is called
   A. alphabetic   B. geographic   C. subject   D. locational

6. Of the following, records management is LEAST concerned with
   A. the development of the best method for retrieving important information
   B. deciding what records should be kept
   C. deciding the number of appointments a client will need
   D. determining the types of folders to be used

7. If records are continually removed from a set of files without "charging" them to the borrower, the filing system will soon become ineffective.
Of the following terms, the one which is NOT applied to a form used in the charge-out system is a
   A. requisition card
   B. out-folder
   C. record retrieval form
   D. substitution card

8. A new clerk has been told to put 500 cards in alphabetical order. Another clerk suggests that she divide the cards into four groups, such as A to F, G to L, M to R, and S to Z, and then alphabetize these four smaller groups.
The suggested method is
   A. *poor*, because the clerk will have to handle the sheets more than once and will waste time
   B. *good*, because it saves time, is more accurate, and is less tiring
   C. *good*, because she will not have to concentrate on it so much when it is in smaller groups
   D. *poor*, because this method is much more tiring than straight alphabetizing

9. In Microsoft Excel, data and records are entered into
   A. pages   B. forms   C. cells   D. contracts

10. Suppose a clerk has been given pads of pre-printed forms to use when taking phone messages for others in her office. The clerk is then observed using scraps of paper and not the forms for writing her messages.
It should be explained that the BEST reason for using the forms is that
   A. they act as a checklist to make sure that the important information is taken
   B. she is expected to do her work in the same way as others in the office
   C. they make sure that unassigned paper is not wasted on phone messages
   D. learning to use these forms will help train her to use more difficult forms

11. The high-speed printing process used for producing large quantities of superior quality copy and cost efficiency is called
   A. photocopying
   B. laser printing
   C. inkjet printing
   D. word processing

12. Of the following, the MAIN reason a stock clerk keeps a perpetual inventory of supplies in the storeroom is that such an inventory will
   A. eliminate the need for a physical inventory
   B. provide a continuous record of supplies on hand
   C. indicate whether a shipment of supplies is satisfactory
   D. dictate the terms of the purchase order

13. As a supervisor, you may be required to handle different types of correspondence.
Of the following types of letters, it would be MOST important to promptly seal which kind of letter?
   A. One marked "confidential"
   B. Those containing enclosures
   C. Any letter to be sent airmail
   D. Those in which copies will be sent along with the original

14. While opening incoming mail, you notice that one letter indicates that an enclosure was to be included but, even after careful inspection, you are not able to find the information to which this refers.
Of the following, the thing that you should do FIRST is
   A. replace the letter in its envelope and return it to the sender
   B. file the letter until the sender's office mails the missing information
   C. type out a letter to the sender informing him of his error
   D. make a notation in the margin of the letter that the enclosure was omitted

15. You have been given a checklist and assigned the responsibility of inspecting certain equipment in the various offices of your agency.
Which of the following is the GREATEST advantage of the checklist?
   A. It indicates which equipment is in greatest demand.
   B. Each piece of equipment on the checklist will be checked only once.
   C. It helps to insure that the equipment listed will not be overlooked.
   D. The equipment listed suggests other equipment you should look for.

16. The BEST way to evaluate the overall state of completion of a construction project is to check the progress estimate against the
   A. inspection worksheet   B. construction schedule
   C. inspector's checklist   D. equipment maintenance schedule

17. The usual contract for agency work includes a section entitled "Instructions to Bidders," which states that the
   A. contractor agrees that he has made his own examination and will make no claim for damages on account of errors or omissions
   B. contractor shall not make claims for damages of any discrepancy, error, or omission in any plans
   C. estimates of quantities and calculations are guaranteed by the agency to be correct and are deemed to be a representation of the conditions affecting the work
   D. plans, measurements, dimensions, and conditions under which the work is to be performed are guaranteed by the agency

18. In order to avoid disputes over payments for extra work in a contract for construction, the BEST procedure to follow would be to
   A. have contractor submit work progress reports daily
   B. insert a special clause in the contract specifications
   C. have a representative on the job at all times to verify conditions
   D. allocate a certain percentage of the cost of the job to cover such expenses

19. Prior to the installation of equipment called for in the specifications, the contractor is USUALLY required to submit for approval
    A. sets of shop drawings
    B. a set of revised specifications
    C. a detailed description of the methods of work to be used
    D. a complete list of skilled and unskilled tradesmen he proposes to use

20. During the actual construction work, the CHIEF value of a construction schedule is to
    A. insure that the work will be done on time
    B. reveal whether production is falling behind
    C. show how much equipment and material is required for the project
    D. furnish data as to the methods and techniques of construction operations

KEY (CORRECT ANSWERS)

1.	B	11.	B
2.	B	12.	B
3.	C	13.	A
4.	C	14.	D
5.	A	15.	C
6.	C	16.	B
7.	C	17.	A
8.	B	18.	C
9.	C	19.	A
10.	A	20.	B

PREPARING WRITTEN MATERIAL
EXAMINATION SECTION
TEST 1

DIRECTIONS: Each of the sentences in this test may be classified under one of the following four categories:
- A. Faulty because of incorrect grammar or word usage
- B. Faulty because of incorrect punctuation
- C. Faulty because of incorrect capitalization or incorrect spelling
- D. Correct

Examine each sentence carefully to determine under which of the above four options it is best classified. Then, in the space to the right, print the capital letter preceding the option which is the BEST of the four suggested above. (Note that each faulty sentence contains but one type of error. Consider a sentence to be correct if it contains none of the types of errors mentioned, even though there may be other correct ways of expressing the same thought.)

1. He sent the notice to the clerk who you hired yesterday.   1.____

2. It must be admitted, however that you were not informed of this change.   2.____

3. Only the employee who have served in this grade for at least two years are eligible for promotion.   3.____

4. The work was divided equally between she and Mary.   4.____

5. He thought that you were not available at that time.   5.____

6. When the messenger returns; please give him this package.   6.____

7. The new secretary prepared, typed, addressed, and delivered, the notices.   7.____

8. Walking into the room, his desk can be seen at the rear.   8.____

9. Although John has worked here longer than She, he produces a smaller amount of work.   9.____

10. She said she could of typed this report yesterday.   10.____

11. Neither one of these procedures are adequate for the efficient performance of this task.   11.____

12. The typewriter is the tool of the typist; the cash register, the tool of the cashier.   12.____

13. "The assignment must be completed as soon as possible" said the supervisor. 13._____

14. As you know, office handbooks are issued to all new Employees. 14._____

15. Writing a speech is sometimes easier than to deliver it before an audience. 15._____

16. Mr. Brown our accountant, will audit the accounts next week. 16._____

17. Give the assignment to whomever is able to do it most efficiently. 17._____

18. The supervisor expected either your or I to file these reports. 18._____

KEY (CORRECT ANSWERS)

1.	A	11.	A
2.	B	12.	C
3.	D	13.	B
4.	A	14.	C
5.	D	15.	A
6.	B	16.	B
7.	B	17.	A
8.	A	18.	A
9.	C		
10.	A		

TEST 2

DIRECTIONS: Each of the sentences in this test may be classified under one of the following four categories:
- A. Faulty because of incorrect grammar or word usage
- B. Faulty because of incorrect punctuation
- C. Faulty because of incorrect capitalization or incorrect spelling
- D. Correct

Examine each sentence carefully to determine under which of the above four options it is best classified. Then, in the space to the right, print the capital letter preceding the option which is the BEST of the four suggested above. (Note that each faulty sentence contains but one type of error. Consider a sentence to be correct if it contains none of the types of errors mentioned, even though there may be other correct ways of expressing the same thought.)

1. The fire apparently started in the storeroom, which is usually locked. 1.____

2. On approaching the victim, two bruises were noticed by this officer. 2.____

3. The officer, who was there examined the report with great care. 3.____

4. Each employee in the office had a seperate desk. 4.____

5. All employees including members of the clerical staff, were invited to the lecture. 5.____

6. The suggested Procedure is similar to the one now in use. 6.____

7. No one was more pleased with the new procedure than the chauffeur. 7.____

8. He tried to persaude her to change the procedure. 8.____

9. The total of the expenses charged to petty cash were high. 9.____

10. An understanding between him and I was finally reached. 10.____

KEY (CORRECT ANSWERS)

1.	D	6.	C
2.	A	7.	D
3.	B	8.	C
4.	C	9.	A
5.	B	10.	A

TEST 3

DIRECTIONS: Each of the sentences in this test may be classified under one of the following four categories:
- A. Faulty because of incorrect grammar or word usage
- B. Faulty because of incorrect punctuation
- C. Faulty because of incorrect capitalization or incorrect spelling
- D. Correct

Examine each sentence carefully to determine under which of the above four options it is best classified. Then, in the space to the right, print the capital letter preceding the option which is the BEST of the four suggested above. (Note that each faulty sentence contains but one type of error. Consider a sentence to be correct if it contains none of the types of errors mentioned, even though there may be other correct ways of expressing the same thought.)

1. They told both he and I that the prisoner had escaped. 1._____

2. Any superior officer, who, disregards the just complaint of his subordinates, is remiss in the performance of his duty. 2._____

3. Only those members of the national organization who resided in the Middle West attended the conference in Chicago. 3._____

4. We told him to give the national organization assignment to whoever was available. 4._____

5. Please do not disappoint and embarass us by not appearing in court. 5._____

6. Although the office's speech proved to be entertaining, the topic was not relevent to the main theme of the conference. 6._____

7. In February all new officers attended a training course in which they were learned in their principal duties and the fundamental operating procedure of the department. 7._____

8. I personally seen inmate Jones threaten inmates Smith and Green with bodily harm if they refused to participate in the plot. 8._____

9. To the layman, who on a chance visit to the prison observes everything functioning smoothly, the maintenance of prison discipline may seem to be a relatively easily realizable objective. 9._____

10. The prisoners in cell block fourty were forbidden to sit on the cell cots during the recreation hour. 10._____

KEY (CORRECT ANSWERS)

1.	A	6.	C
2.	B	7.	A
3.	C	8.	A
4.	D	9.	D
5.	C	10.	C

TEST 4

DIRECTIONS: Each of the sentences in this test may be classified under one of the following four categories:
  A. Faulty because of incorrect grammar or word usage
  B. Faulty because of incorrect punctuation
  C. Faulty because of incorrect capitalization or incorrect spelling
  D. Correct

Examine each sentence carefully to determine under which of the above four options it is best classified. Then, in the space to the right, print the capital letter preceding the option which is the BEST of the four suggested above. (Note that each faulty sentence contains but one type of error. Consider a sentence to be correct if it contains none of the types of errors mentioned, even though there may be other correct ways of expressing the same thought.)

1. I cannot encourage you any.   1._____
2. You always look well in those sort of clothes.   2._____
3. Shall we go to the park?   3._____
4. The man whome he introduced was Mr. Carey.   4._____
5. She saw the letter laying here this morning.   5._____
6. It should rain before the Afternoon is over.   6._____
7. They have already went home.   7._____
8. That Jackson will be elected is evident.   8._____
9. He does not hardly approve of us.   9._____
10. It was he, who won the prize.   10._____

KEY (CORRECT ANSWERS)

1.	A	6.	C
2.	A	7.	A
3.	D	8.	D
4.	C	9.	A
5.	A	10.	B

TEST 5

DIRECTIONS: Each of the sentences in this test may be classified under one of the following four categories:
- A. Faulty because of incorrect grammar or word usage
- B. Faulty because of incorrect punctuation
- C. Faulty because of incorrect capitalization or incorrect spelling
- D. Correct

Examine each sentence carefully to determine under which of the above four options it is best classified. Then, in the space to the right, print the capital letter preceding the option which is the BEST of the four suggested above. (Note that each faulty sentence contains but one type of error. Consider a sentence to be correct if it contains none of the types of errors mentioned, even though there may be other correct ways of expressing the same thought.)

1. Shall we go to the park.   1.____
2. They are, alike, in this particular way.   2.____
3. They gave the poor man sume food when he knocked on the door.   3.____
4. I regret the loss caused by the error.   4.____
5. The students' will have a new teacher.   5.____
6. They sweared to bring out all the facts.   6.____
7. He decided to open a branch store on 33rd street.   7.____
8. His speed is equal and more than that of a racehorse.   8.____
9. He felt very warm on that Summer day.   9.____
10. He was assisted by his friend, who lives in the next house.   10.____

KEY (CORRECT ANSWERS)

1.	B	6.	A
2.	B	7.	C
3.	C	8.	A
4.	D	9.	C
5.	B	10.	D

TEST 6

DIRECTIONS: Each of the sentences in this test may be classified under one of the following four categories:
- A. Faulty because of incorrect grammar or word usage
- B. Faulty because of incorrect punctuation
- C. Faulty because of incorrect capitalization or incorrect spelling
- D. Correct

Examine each sentence carefully to determine under which of the above four options it is best classified. Then, in the space to the right, print the capital letter preceding the option which is the BEST of the four suggested above. (Note that each faulty sentence contains but one type of error. Consider a sentence to be correct if it contains none of the types of errors mentioned, even though there may be other correct ways of expressing the same thought.)

1. The climate of New York is colder than California. 1.____
2. I shall wait for you on the corner. 2.____
3. Did we see the boy who, we think, is the leader. 3.____
4. Being a modest person, John seldom talks about his invention. 4.____
5. The gang is called the smith street bos. 5.____
6. He seen the man break into the store. 6.____
7. We expected to lay still there for quite a while. 7.____
8. He is considered to be the Leader of his organization. 8.____
9. Although I recieved an invitation, I won't go. 9.____
10. The letter must be here some place. 10.____

KEY (CORRECT ANSWERS)

1.	A	6.	A
2.	D	7.	A
3.	B	8.	C
4.	D	9.	C
5.	C	10.	A

TEST 7

DIRECTIONS: Each of the sentences in this test may be classified under one of the following four categories:
- A. Faulty because of incorrect grammar or word usage
- B. Faulty because of incorrect punctuation
- C. Faulty because of incorrect capitalization or incorrect spelling
- D. Correct

Examine each sentence carefully to determine under which of the above four options it is best classified. Then, in the space to the right, print the capital letter preceding the option which is the BEST of the four suggested above. (Note that each faulty sentence contains but one type of error. Consider a sentence to be correct if it contains none of the types of errors mentioned, even though there may be other correct ways of expressing the same thought.)

1. I though it to be he. 1.____
2. We expect to remain here for a long time. 2.____
3. The committee was agreed. 3.____
4. Two-thirds of the building are finished. 4.____
5. The water was froze. 5.____
6. Everyone of the salesmen must supply their own car. 6.____
7. Who is the author of Gone With the Wind? 7.____
8. He marched on and declaring that he would never surrender. 8.____
9. Who shall I say called? 9.____
10. Everyone has left but they. 10.____

KEY (CORRECT ANSWERS)

1. A   6. A
2. D   7. B
3. D   8. A
4. A   9. D
5. A   10. D

TEST 8

DIRECTIONS: Each of the sentences in this test may be classified under one of the following four categories:
- A. Faulty because of incorrect grammar or word usage
- B. Faulty because of incorrect punctuation
- C. Faulty because of incorrect capitalization or incorrect spelling
- D. Correct

Examine each sentence carefully to determine under which of the above four options it is best classified. Then, in the space to the right, print the capital letter preceding the option which is the BEST of the four suggested above. (Note that each faulty sentence contains but one type of error. Consider a sentence to be correct if it contains none of the types of errors mentioned, even though there may be other correct ways of expressing the same thought.)

1. Who did we give the order to? 1.____
2. Send your order in immediately. 2.____
3. I believe I paid the Bill. 3.____
4. I have not met but one person. 4.____
5. Why aren't Tom, and Fred, going to the dance? 5.____
6. What reason is there for him not going? 6.____
7. The seige of Malta was a tremendous event. 7.____
8. I was there yesterday I assure you 8.____
9. Your ukulele is better than mine. 9.____
10. No one was there only Mary. 10.____

KEY (CORRECT ANSWERS)

1. A   6. A
2. D   7. C
3. C   8. B
4. A   9. C
5. B   10. A

TEST 9

DIRECTIONS: In each of the following groups of sentences, one of the four sentences is faulty in grammar, punctuation, or capitalization. Select the INCORRECT sentence in each case.

1. A. If you had stood at home and done your homework, you would not have failed in arithmetic.
   B. Her affected manner annoyed every member of the audience.
   C. How will the new law affect our income taxes?
   D. The plants were not affected by the long, cold winter, but they succumbed to the drought of summer.

   1.____

2. A. He is one of the most able men who have been in the Senate.
   B. It is he who is to blame for the lamentable mistake.
   C. Haven't you a helpful suggestion to make at this time?
   D. The money was robbed from the blind man's cup.

   2.____

3. A. The amount of children in this school is steadily increasing.
   B. After taking an apple from the table, she went out to play.
   C. He borrowed a dollar from me.
   D. I had hoped my brother would arrive before me.

   3.____

4. A. Whom do you think I hear from every week?
   B. Who do you think is the right man for the job?
   C. Who do you think I found in the room?
   D. He is the man whom we considered a good candidate for the presidency.

   4.____

5. A. Quietly the puppy laid down before the fireplace.
   B. You have made your bed; now lie in it.
   C. I was badly sunburned because I had lain too long in the sun.
   D. I laid the doll on the bed and left the room.

   5.____

KEY (CORRECT ANSWERS)

1. A
2. D
3. A
4. C
5. A

MECHANICAL APTITUDE
TOOL RECOGNITION AND USE
EXAMINATION SECTION
TEST 1

DIRECTIONS: Each question or incomplete statement is followed by several suggested answers or completions. Select the one that BEST answers the question or completes the statement. *PRINT THE LETTER OF THE CORRECT ANSWER IN THE SPACE AT THE RIGHT.*

Questions 1-16.

DIRECTIONS: Questions 1 through 16 refer to the tools shown below. The numbers in the answers refer to the numbers below the tools. NOTE: These tools are NOT shown to scale.

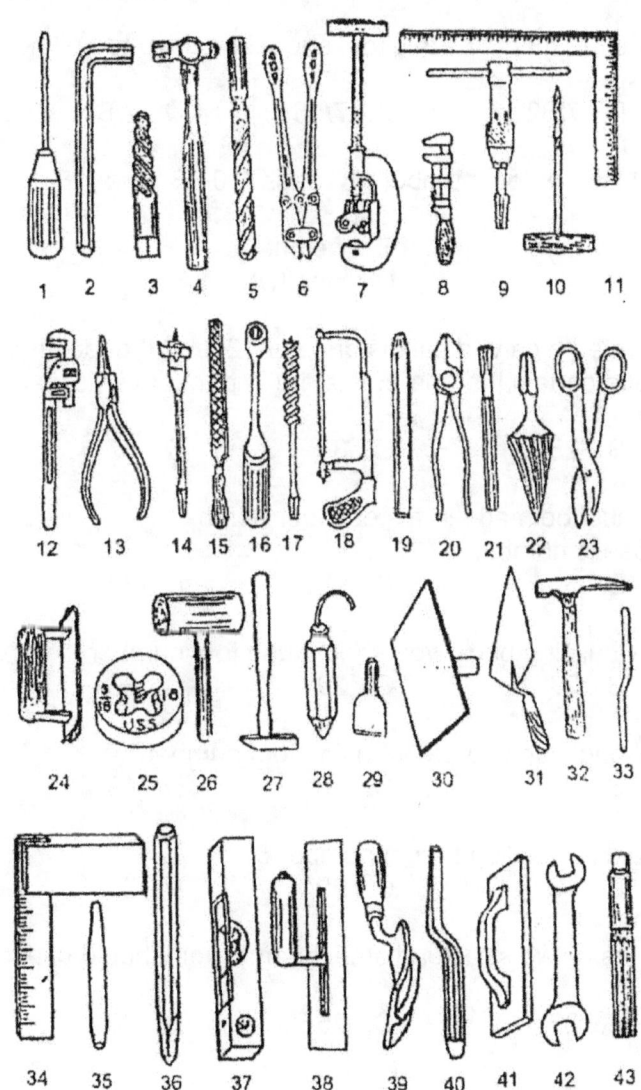

2 (#1)

1. In order to cut a piece of 5/16" diameter steel scaffold hoisting cable, you should use tool number
    A. 6 B. 7 C. 19 D. 23

    1.____

2. Scaffold planks are secured to joisting irons by means of lag screws.
   To properly tighten these lag screws, you should use tool number
    A. 12 B. 13 C. 20 D. 42

    2.____

3. While installing a steel angle iron lintel, you find that the threads on the embedded holding bolts are damaged.
   You should repair the threads by using tool number
    A. 7 B. 9 C. 25 D. 43

    3.____

4. It is necessary to cut a hole in a concrete foundation wall in order to place a small bolt.
   To cut this small hole, you should use tool number
    A. 14 B. 19 C. 21 D. 40

    4.____

5. If tool number 17 bears the mark "7," this tool should be used to drill holes having a diameter of
    A. 7/64" B. 7/32" C. 7/16" D. 7/8"

    5.____

6. If the marking on the blade of tool number 18 reads "10-18," the "18" refers to the
    A. number of teeth per inch   B. weight
    C. thickness   D. length

    6.____

7. If two points are separated by a vertical distance of 12 feet, the tool that should be used to make certain that the points are in perfect vertical alignment is number
    A. 11 B. 28 C. 34 D. 37

    7.____

8. A 3/4" diameter hole must be made in a steel floor beam.
   The tool you should use is number
    A. 3 B. 5 C. 9 D. 22

    8.____

9. To cut the corner off a building brick, you should use tool number
    A. 4 B. 27 C. 29 D. 36

    9.____

10. A 2" x 2" x 3/16" steel angle should be cut using tool number
    A. 6 B. 7 C. 18 D. 19

    10.____

11. The term "snips" should be applied to tool number
    A. 6 B. 13 C. 20 D. 23

    11.____

12. To line-up the bolt holes in two structural steel beams, you should use tool number
    A. 1 B. 33 C. 35 D. 36

    12.____

13. A "hawk" is tool number 13.____
    A. 29 B. 30 C. 38 D. 41

14. After an 8" thick brick wall has been erected, it is discovered that a hole 14.____
    should have been left for a 4" sewer pipe.
    To cut that hole, you should use tool number
    A. 5 B. 19 C. 32 D. 36

15. A "float" is tool number 15.____
    A. 30 B. 31 C. 33 D. 41

16. A "Stillson" is tool number 16.____
    A. 2 B. 8 C. 12 D. 22

KEY (CORRECT ANSWERS)

1. A 11. D
2. D 12. C
3. C 13. B
4. C 14. D
5. C 15. D

6. A 16. C
7. B
8. B
9. C
10. C

TEST 2

DIRECTIONS: Each question or incomplete statement is followed by several suggested answers or completions. Select the one that BEST answers the question or completes the statement. *PRINT THE LETTER OF THE CORRECT ANSWER IN THE SPACE AT THE RIGHT.*

1. The stake shown in the sketch at the right is a _____ stake.
    A. hatchet
    B. conductor
    C. solid mandrel
    D. beak horn

    1.____

2. When a circle is too large to be drawn with a pair of dividers, the PROPER tool to use is a
    A. trammel
    B. protractor
    C. combination set
    D. flexible curve

    2.____

3. A rivet set is a tool used to
    A. shape the head of a rivet
    B. mark off the spacing of rivets
    C. remove a loose rivet
    D. check the shank length of a rivet

    3.____

4. The hammer shown in the sketch at the right is a _____ hammer.
    A. raising
    B. ball peen
    C. setting
    D. cross-over

    4.____

5. Of the following, the BEST tool to use to scribe a line parallel to the straight edge of a piece of sheet metal is a(n)
    A. outside caliper
    B. pair of dividers
    C. template
    D. scratch gage

    5.____

6. Of the following, the BEST device to use to check the condition of the insulation of a cable is the
    A. ohmmeter
    B. wheatstone bridge
    C. voltmeter
    D. megger

    6.____

7. Of the following fittings, the one used to connect two lengths of conduit in a straight line is a(n)
    A. elbow   B. nipple   C. tee   D. coupling

    7.____

8. If a nut is to be tightened to an exact specified value, the wrench that should be used is a(n) _____ wrench.
    A. torque   B. lock-jaw   C. alligator   D. spaner

    8.____

9. A stillson wrench is also called a _____ wrench. 9.____
    A. strap   B. pipe   C. monkey   D. crescent

10. A machine screw is indicated on a drawing as . 10.____
    The head is the American Standard type called
    A. flat
    B. oval
    C. fillister
    D. round

11. The tool that is shown at the right is properly 11.____
    referred to as a(n) _____ tap.
    A. bottoming
    B. acme
    C. taper
    D. plug

12. The tool indicated at the right is referred to as 12.____
    an Arc Punch. This tool should be used to
    A. cut holes in 1/16" steel
    B. cut large diameter holes in masonry
    C. run through a conduit prior to pulling a cable or wires
    D. make holes in rubber or leather gasket material

13. The plumbing fitting shown at the right is called a 13.____
    A. street elbow
    B. return bend
    C. running trap
    D. reversing "el"

14. For which one of the following uses would it be unsafe to use a carpenter's 14.____
    hammer?
    A. casing nail   B. hand punch
    C. hardened steel surface D. plastic surface

15. Of the following, the MAIN advantage in using a Phillips head screw is that 15.____
    A. the threads of the Phillips head screw have a deeper bite than standard screw threads
    B. the screwdriver used on this type of screw is more likely to keep its edge than a standard screwdriver
    C. a single screwdriver fits all size screws of this type
    D. the screwdriver used on this type of screw is less likely to slip than a standard screwdriver

16. One of the reasons why a polyester rope is considered to be the BEST general purpose rope is that it
    A. does not stretch as much as ropes made of other materials
    B. is available in longer lengths than ropes made of other materials
    C. does not fray as much as ropes made of other materials
    D. contains more strands than ropes made of other materials

16._____

17. The PROPER saw to use to cut wood with the grain is a _____ saw.
    A. hack   B. crosscut   C. back   D. rip

17._____

18. Assume that the instruction manual for a machine indicates that a certain bolt must be tightened with a specified amount of force.
    Of the following tools, the one which should be used to tighten the bolt with the specified amount of force is a(n) _____ wrench.
    A. torque   B. adjustable   C. stillson   D combination

18._____

19. The power source of a pneumatic tool is
    A. manual
    B. water pressure
    C. compressed air
    D. electricity

19._____

20. The tool used to cut internal pipe threads is a
    A. broach   B. tap   C. die   D. rod

20._____

KEY (CORRECT ANSWERS)

1.	A	11.	A
2.	A	12.	D
3.	A	13.	B
4.	C	14.	C
5.	D	15.	D
6.	D	16.	A
7.	D	17.	D
8.	A	18.	A
9.	B	19.	C
10.	B	20.	B

ABSTRACT REASONING

COMMENTARY

Since intelligence exists in many forms or phases and the theory of differential aptitudes is now firmly established in testing, other manifestations and measurements of intelligence than verbal or purely arithmetical must be identified and measured.

Classification inventory, or figure classification, involves the aptitude of form perception, i.e., the ability to perceive pertinent detail in objects or in pictorial or graphic material. It involves making visual comparisons and discriminations and discerning slight differences in shapes and shading figures and widths and lengths of lines.

Leading examples of presentation are the figure analogy and the figure classification. The section that follows presents progressive and varied samplings of this type of question.

SAMPLE QUESTIONS

DIRECTIONS: In each of these sample questions, look at the symbols in the first two boxes. Something about the three symbols in the first box makes them alike; something about the two symbols in the other box with the question mark makes them alike. Look for some characteristic that is common to all symbols in the same box, yet makes them different from the symbols in the other box. Among the five answer choices, find the symbol that can BEST be substituted for the question mark, because it is *like* the symbols in the second box, and, for the same reason, different from those in the first box.

1.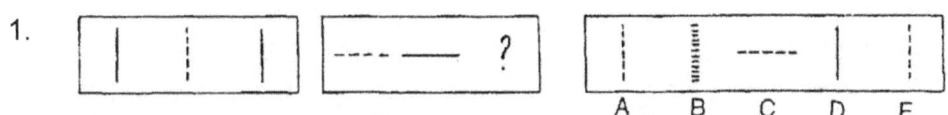

In sample question 1, all the symbols in the first box are vertical lines. The second box has two lines, one broken and one solid. Their *likeness* to each other consists in their being horizontal; and their being horizontal makes them *different* from the vertical lines in the other box. The answer must be the only one of the five lettered choices that is a horizontal line, ether broken or solid. Therefore, the CORRECT answer is C.

2.

The CORRECT answer is A.

EXAMINATION SECTION
TEST 1

DIRECTIONS: In each of these questions, look at the symbols in the first two boxes. Something about the three symbols in the first box makes them alike; something about the two symbols in the other box with the question mark makes them alike. Look for some characteristic that is common to all symbols in the same box, yet makes them different from the symbols in the other box. Among the five answer choices, find the symbol that can BEST be substituted for the question mark, because it is *like* the symbols in the second box, and, for the same reason, different from those in the first box. PRINT THE LETTER OF THE CORRECT ANSWER IN THE SPACE AT THE RIGHT.

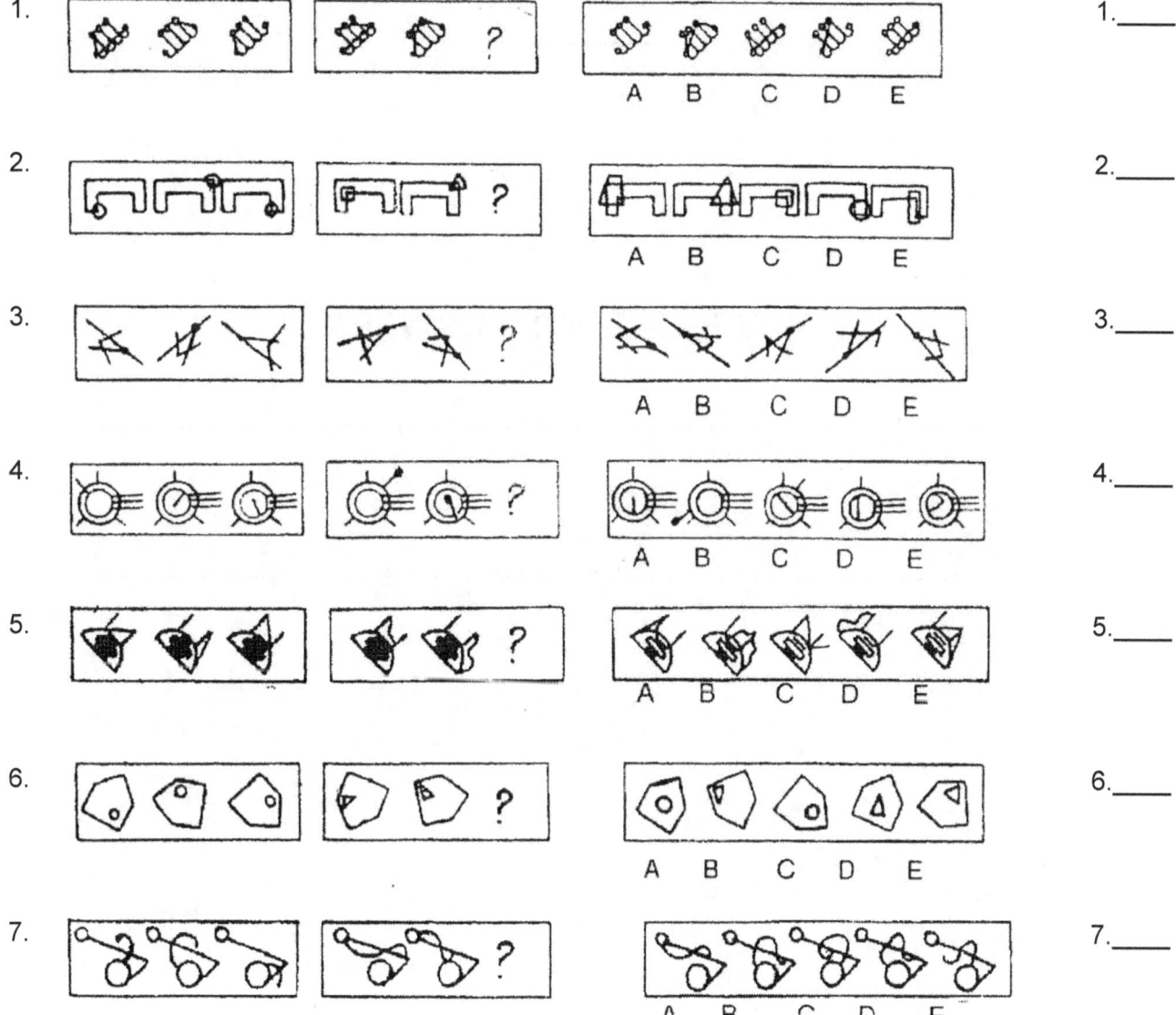

1.____

2.____

3.____

4.____

5.____

6.____

7.____

2 (#1)

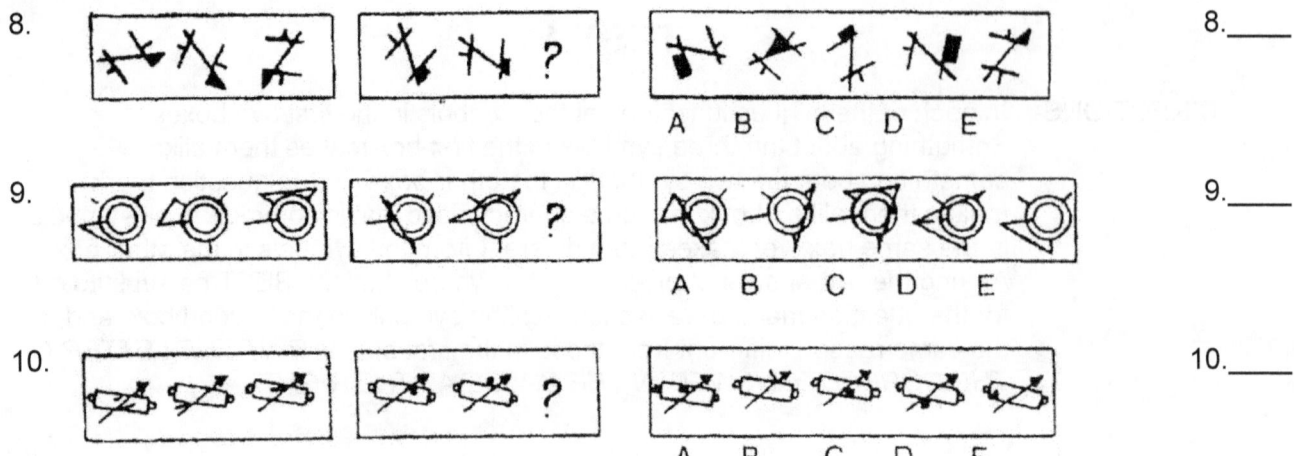

KEY (CORRECT ANSWERS)

1.	B	6.	B
2.	C	7.	A
3.	C	8.	C
4.	B	9.	B
5.	D	10.	D

TEST 2

DIRECTIONS: In each of these questions, look at the symbols in the first two boxes. Something about the three symbols in the first box makes them alike; something about the two symbols in the other box with the question mark makes them alike. Look for some characteristic that is common to all symbols in the same box, yet makes them different from the symbols in the other box. Among the five answer choices, find the symbol that can BEST be substituted for the question mark, because it is *like* the symbols in the second box, and, for the same reason, different from those in the first box. *PRINT THE LETTER OF THE CORRECT ANSWER IN THE SPACE AT THE RIGHT.*

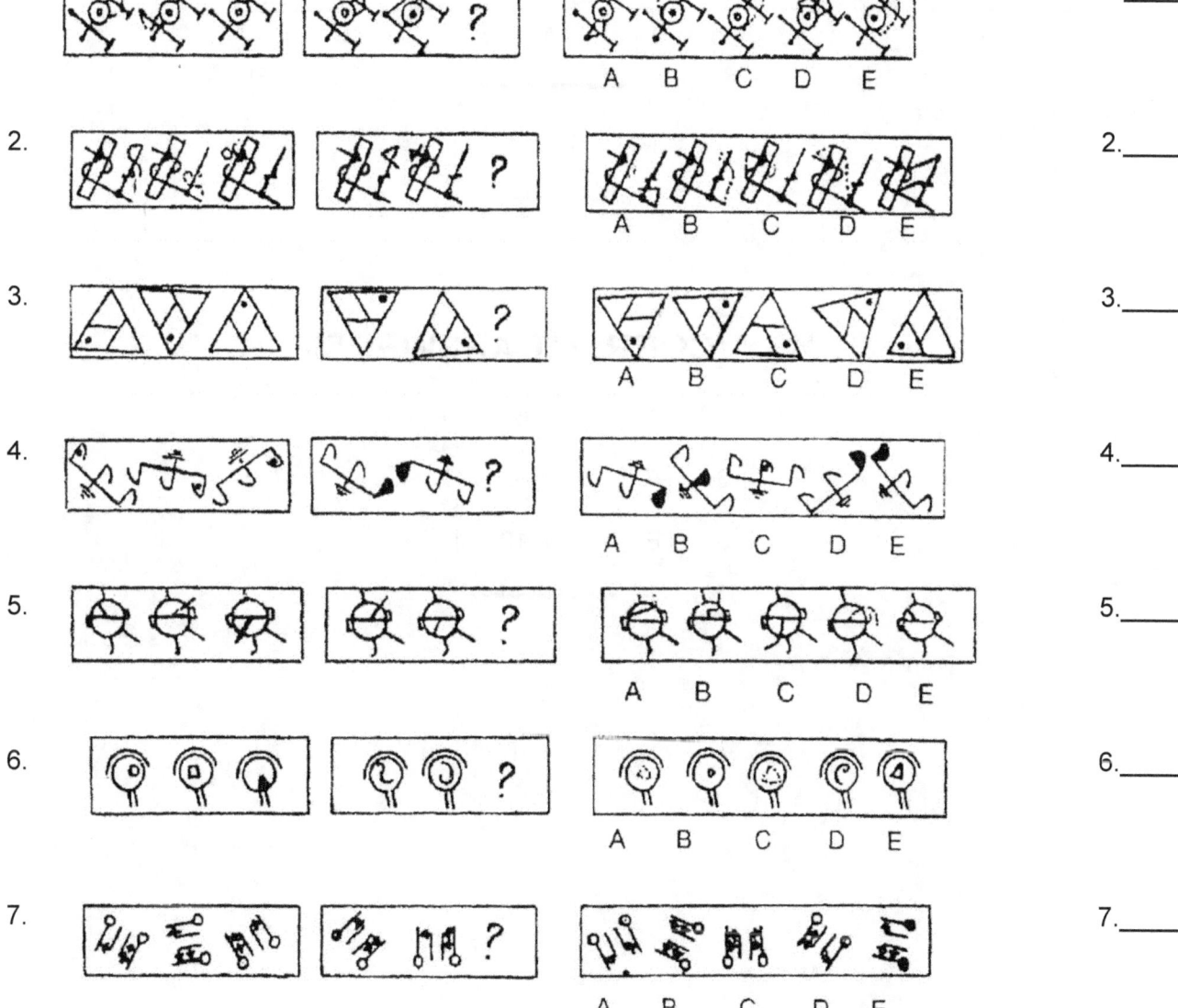

1._____

2._____

3._____

4._____

5._____

6._____

7._____

119

8.

9.

10.

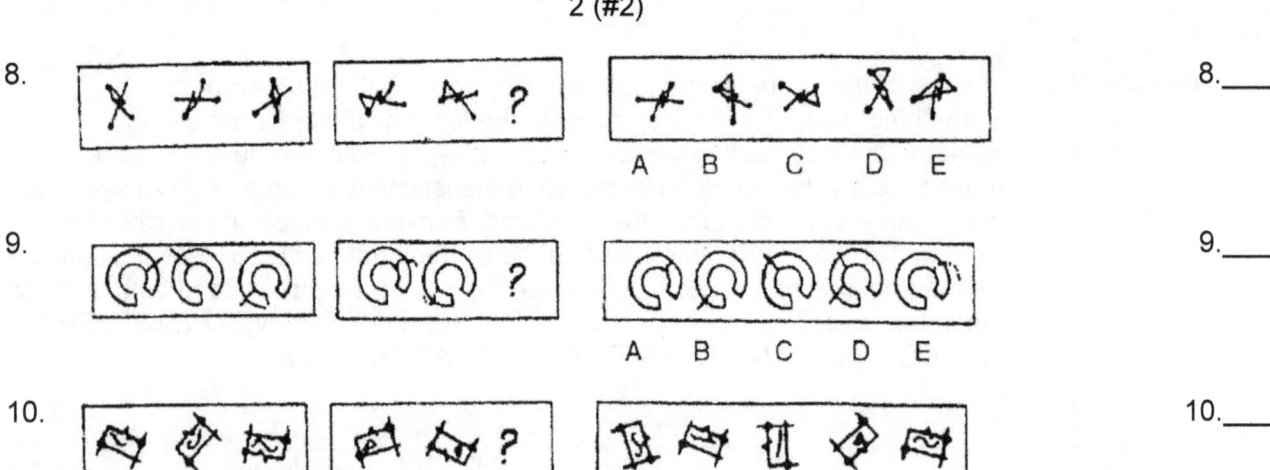

KEY (CORRECT ANSWERS)

1.	A	6.	D
2.	A	7.	D
3.	A	8.	C
4.	D	9.	E
5.	E	10.	D

TEST 3

DIRECTIONS: In each of these questions, look at the symbols in the first two boxes. Something about the three symbols in the first box makes them alike; something about the two symbols in the other box with the question mark makes them alike. Look for some characteristic that is common to all symbols in the same box, yet makes them different from the symbols in the other box. Among the five answer choices, find the symbol that can BEST be substituted for the question mark, because it is *like* the symbols in the second box, and, for the same reason, different from those in the first box. PRINT THE LETTER OF THE CORRECT ANSWER IN THE SPACE AT THE RIGHT.

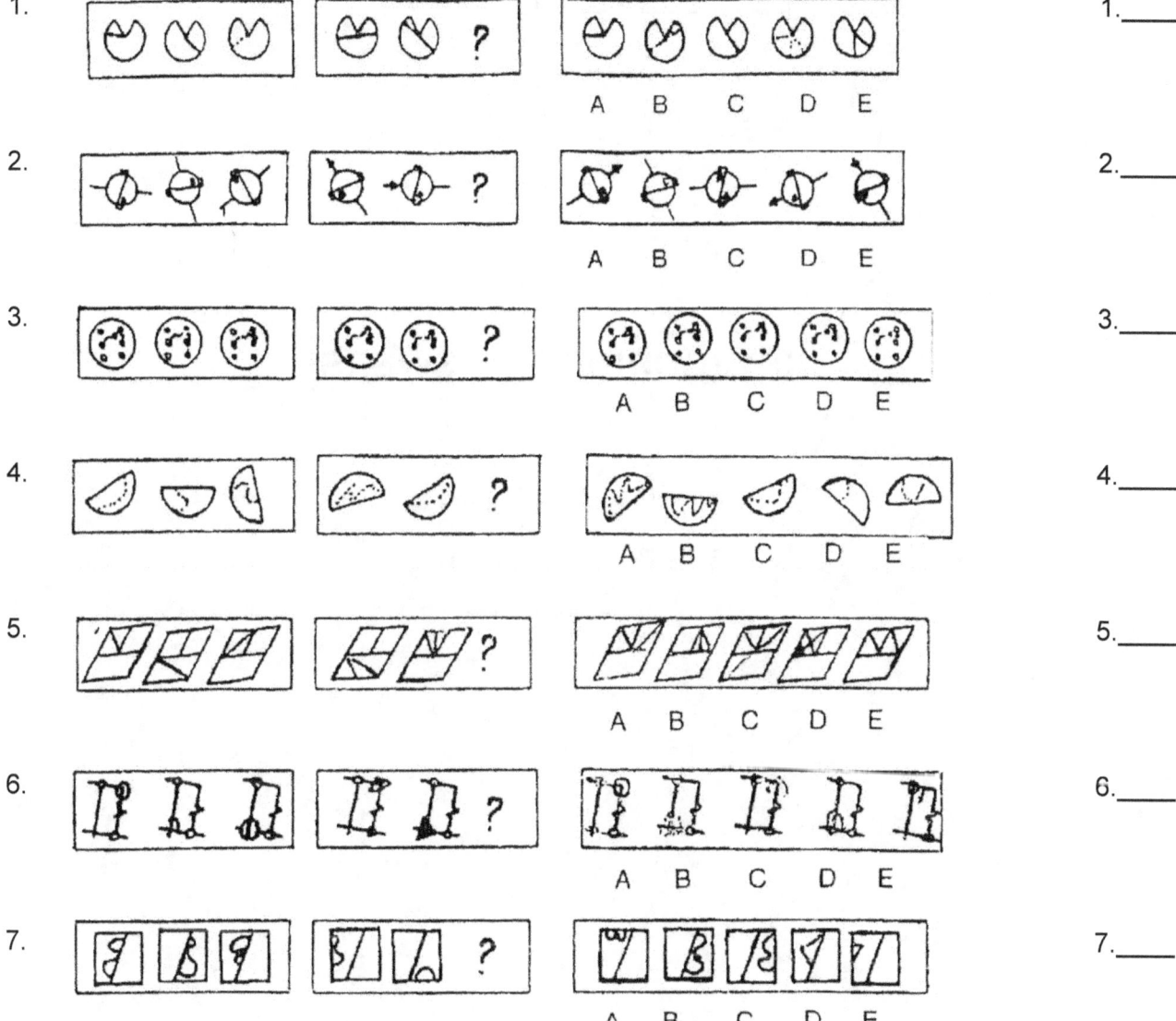

1.____

2.____

3.____

4.____

5.____

6.____

7.____

121

2 (#3)

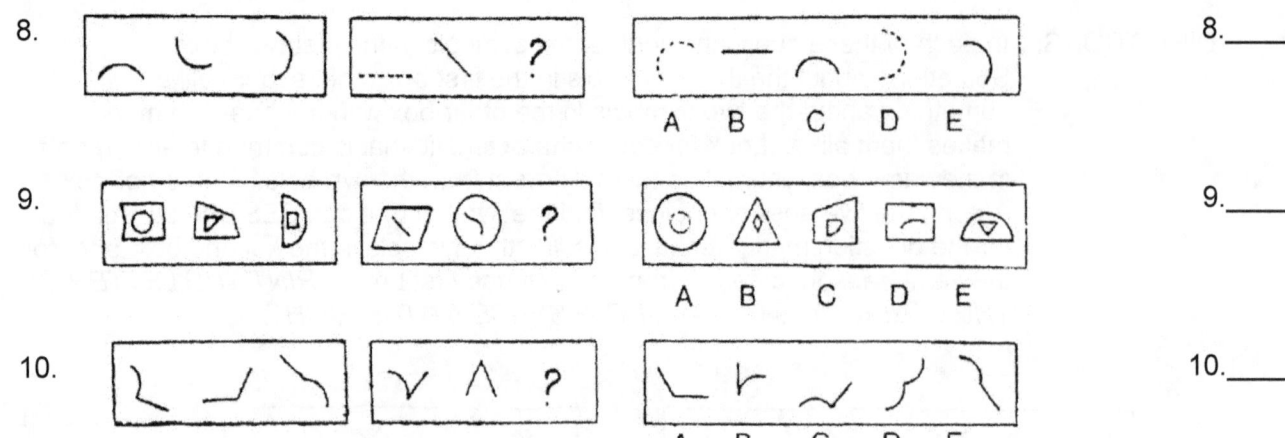

KEY (CORRECT ANSWERS)

1.	B	6.	C
2.	E	7.	C
3.	C	8.	B
4.	A	9.	D
5.	B	10.	B

NUMBER AND LETTER SERIES

COMMENTARY

One of the most searching types of the arithmetic reasoning question—a basic staple of tests of general and mental ability—is the number-series problem, in which a series of single numbers (or paired numbers) is presented, which follow a certain rule or sequence. The examinee is to select the next number (or pair of numbers) if the series were to be continued in this manner.

More difficult still, and on the highest level of difficulty is the letter-series question, wherein a series of letters, instead of numbers, is to be followed according to a definite order. Here, the element of abstractness serves to add further complexity to the problem.

Suggestion: In solving alphabetic series and progressions, it is wise to write out the alphabet and keep it in front of you. With this visual and aid immediately available, the key to each series can then be solved much more easily that way.

The questions in this section test your ability to see relationships between the elements of a series. These questions are sometimes referred to as series or progressions, and, in them, the candidate is asked to determine the rule that binds the elements together and then select the following element(s) according to that rule.

NUMBER SERIES/ONE NUMBER

SAMPLE QUESTIONS

DIRECTIONS: Each of the three sample questions presents a series of six numbers. Each series of numbers is made up according to a certain rule or order. You are to find what the next number in the series should be if the series were to be continued in this sequence.

1. 2 4 6 8 10 12
   A. 14 B. 16 C. 18
   D. 20 E. None of the above

   1.____

Explanation: In Question 1, the rule is to add 2 to each number (2+2 = 4; 4 + 2 = 6, etc.). The net number in the series is 14 (12+2 = 14). Since 14 is lettered A among the suggested answers, A is the correct answer.

2. 7 8 6 7 5 6
   A. 2 B. 3 C. 4
   D. 5 E. None of the above

   2.____

Explanation: In Question 2, the rule is to add 1 to the first number, subtract 2 from the next, add 1, subtract 2, and so on. The next number in the series is 4; letter C is the correct answer.

3. 3 6 9 12 15 18

   3.____

Explanation: In Question 3, the rule is to add 3, making 21 the next number in the series. The correct answer to Question 3 is *none of the above*, since 39, 40, 45, and 59 are all incorrect answers; therefore, E is the correct answer.

NUMBER SERIES/ONE NUMBER
EXAMINATION SECTION
TEST 1

DIRECTIONS: Each of the following questions presents a series of single numbers. Five possible answers are given. From these choices, you are to find what the next number in the series should be if the series were to be continued in this sequence. *PRINT THE LETTER OF THE CORRECT ANSWER IN THE SPACE AT THE RIGHT.*

1. 3 13 4 15 5 7 6 19 7
   A. 20   B. 23   C. 21   D. 25   D. 27   1.____

2. 20 25 23 28 26 31 29 34
   A. 33   B. 32   C. 31   D. 30   E. 34   2.____

3. 9 24 39 54 69 84 99 114
   A. 129   B. 124   C. 128   D. 130   E. 126   3.____

4. 20 29 37 44 50 55 59
   A. 61   B. 62   C. 63   D. 64   E. 66   4.____

5. 20 21 23 26 30 35 41 48
   A. 55   B. 56   C. 54   D. 59   E. 57   5.____

6. 8 10 14 20 28 38 50 64
   A. 80   B. 72   C. 71   D. 73   E. 75   6.____

7. 6 7 9 12 16 21 28 35
   A. 40   B. 47   C. 50   D. 45   E. 43   7.____

8. 8 11 16 24 34 47
   A. 61   B. 62   C. 55   D. 60   E. 63   8.____

9. 3 8 14 25 37 54
   A. 67   B. 69   C. 68   D. 70   E. 72   9.____

10. 5 15 23 29 39 47 53 63
    A. 71   B. 72   C. 69   D. 73   E. 70   10.____

KEY (CORRECT ANSWERS)

1. C   6. A
2. B   7. E
3. A   8. B
4. B   9. E
5. B   10. A

TEST 2

DIRECTIONS: Each of the following questions presents a series of single numbers. Five possible answers are given. From these choices, you are to find what the next number in the series should be if the series were to be continued in this sequence. *PRINT THE LETTER OF THE CORRECT ANSWER IN THE SPACE AT THE RIGHT.*

1. 2 4 8 16 32 64 128
   A. 228   B. 130   C. 248   D. 264   E. 256

   1.____

2. 4 8 16 24 32 40 48
   A. 64   B. 56   C. 96   D. 62   E. 84

   2.____

3. 2 4 4 8 8 16 16
   A. 54   B. 48   C. 16   D. 32   E. 36

   3.____

4. 3 6 18 36 108 216 648
   A. 1946   B. 1944   C. 1296   D. 1056   E. 1488

   4.____

5. 10 13 11 14 12 15 13
   A. 14   B. 11   C. 15   D. 17   E. 16

   5.____

6. 2 6 18 54 162 486
   A. 1556   B. 496   C. 1286   D. 1458   E. 1552

   6.____

7. 4 20 35 49 62 74
   A. 82   B. 85   C. 93   D. 94   E. 96

   7.____

8. 10 15 12 17 14 19
   A. 22   B. 24   C. 21   D. 14   E. 16

   8.____

9. 4 10 8 14 12 18
   A. 16   B. 20   C. 24   D. 22   E. 21

   9.____

10. 10 18 15 23 20 28
    A. 23   B. 24   C. 25   D. 36   E. 40

    10.____

KEY (CORRECT ANSWERS)

1.	E	6.	D
2.	B	7.	B
3.	D	8.	E
4.	C	9.	A
5.	E	10.	C

TEST 3

NUMBER SERIES/TWO NUMBERS

SAMPLE QUESTIONS

DIRECTIONS: These questions are more difficult. In these, the arrangement is more complicated, and the answer is chosen from groups of two numbers, of which one group gives the next two numbers in the series

1. 1 1 2 1 3 1 4
   A. 15   B. 41   C. 51   D. 55   E. 61

1.____

Explanation: The series consists of 1's alternating with numbers in ascending numerical order. The next two numbers would be 5 and 1. Therefore, C is the correct answer.

2. 2 8 3 7 5 6 8 5
   A. 106   B. 113   C. 114   D. 124   E. 126

2.____

Explanation: This series consists of a sub-series for which the rule is to add 1, add 2, add 3, and add 4, alternating with another series in descending numerical order. The next number in the first sub-series would be 8 + 4, or 12; and the next number in the descending series would be 4. Therefore, D is the correct answer.

DIRECTIONS: Each of the following questions presents a series of single numbers. Five possible answers are given. From these choices, you are to find what the next number in the series should be if the series were to be continued in this sequence. *PRINT THE LETTER OF THE CORRECT ANSWER IN THE SPACE AT THE RIGHT.*

1. 3 4 3 5 3 6 3 7 3
   A. 8 3   B. 9 3   C. 9 4   D. 4 8   E. 7 5

1.____

2. 50 2 48 4 6 6 44
   A. 846   B. 842   C. 428   D. 448   E. 844

2.____

3. 40 39 43 38 6 37 49 36
   A. 3751   B. 3952   C. 5137   D. 3552   E. 5235

3.____

4. 50 51 49 53 47 56 44 60 40
   A. 6040   B. 3560   C. 6035   D. 6535   E. 3565

4.____

5. 1 100 2 50 4 25 8
   A. 12.54   B. 12.516   C. 16 12.5   D. 8.25 16   E. 16 8.25

5.____

6. 1 25 2 24 4 22 7 19 11
   A. 15 16   B. 16 16   C. 16 15   D. 18 17   E. 17 18

6.____

7. 2 4 6 8 12 14 18 20
   A. 26 22   B. 26 24   C. 22 26   D. 21 24   E. 24 26

7.____

2 (#3)

8. 1 2 4 8 16 32
    A. 48 64   B. 64 128   C. 64 72   D. 63 129   E. 72 64   8._____

9. 10 50 13 54 16 58 19 62
    A. 22 66   B. 66 22   C. 64 20   D. 66 20   E. 20 66   9._____

10. 2 60 12 58 22 56 32
    A. 36 46   B. 42 54   C. 56 42   D. 42 56   E. 54 42   10._____

11. 2 90 4 80 6 70 8 60
    A. 12 52   B. 50 10   C. 10 50   D. 12 50   E. 50 12   11._____

12. 10 70 11 67 13 64 16 61
    A. 19 58   B. 20 58   C. 18 58   D. 58 20   E. 58 19   12._____

13. 10 20 30 12 23 26 14 26 22 16
    A. 19 29   B. 29 18   C. 29 19   D. 18 29   E. 30 18   13._____

14. 2 5 4 6 8 8 14 11 22 15
    A. 32 20   B. 30 20   C. 20 32   D. 31 21   E. 20 30   14._____

15. 10 15 20 11 17 23 12 19 26 13 21 29 14
    A. 16 29   B. 15 23   C. 23 32   D. 32 23   E. 23 15   15._____

KEY (CORRECT ANSWERS)

1.	A	6.	A	11.	C
2.	B	7.	E	12.	B
3.	E	8.	B	13.	B
4.	D	9.	A	14.	A
5.	B	10.	E	15.	C

TEST 4

DIRECTIONS: Each of the following questions presents a series of single numbers. Five possible answers are given. From these choices, you are to find what the next number in the series should be if the series were to be continued in this sequence. *PRINT THE LETTER OF THE CORRECT ANSWER IN THE SPACE AT THE RIGHT.*

1. 150 120 149 118 147 114 044 108 140
   A. 104 138   B. 102 136   C. 135 140   D. 100 135   E. 135 100

   1.____

2. 10 11 12 11 12 13 12 13 14 13 14 15 14
   A. 15 16   B. 13 14   C. 14 15   D. 16 15   E. 15 14

   2.____

3. 2 4 5 6 11 10 20 16 32 24
   A. 34 46   B. 32 46   C. 48 32   D. 46 32   E. 47 34

   3.____

4. 1 2 3 2 4 6 3 6 9 4 8 12 5
   A. 9 15   B. 9 14   C. 11 16   D. 10 14   E. 10 15

   4.____

5. 1 2 3 4 4 4 7 6 5 10 86
   A. 10 13   B. 13 10   C. 12 10   D. 12 9   E. 10 9

   5.____

6. 1 2 3 5 5 7 9 8 11 13 11
   A. 15 17   B. 17 15   C. 18 15   D. 15 18   E. 16 18

   6.____

7. 10 12 13 14 15 17 18 19 20 22
   A. 23 24   B. 24 23   C. 23 23   D. 22 24   E. 24 22

   7.____

8. 2 3 4 4 8 6 10 7 14 9 16 10 20 12
   A. 13 22   B. 12 24   C. 20 12   D. 24 12   E. 22 13

   8.____

9. 1 2 2 5 4 9 5 12 7 16 8 19 10 23
   A. 27 12   B. 12 27   C. 11 26   D. 26 11   E. 12 28

   9.____

10. 100 106 98 103 97 99 95 96 94 92 92 89 91 85
    A. 82 89   B. 89 82   C. 90 81   D. 81 90   E. 90 83

    10.____

KEY (CORRECT ANSWERS)

1.	D	6.	A
2.	A	7.	A
3.	E	8.	E
4.	E	9.	C
5.	B	10.	B

TEST 5

LETTER SERIES

SAMPLE QUESTIONS

DIRECTIONS: In each of these questions, there is a series of letters which follow some definite order, and underneath there are five sets of two letters each. Look at the letters in the series and determine what the order is; then, from the suggested answers below, select the set that gives the next two letters in the series in their correct order.

1. X C X D X E X
   A. F X   B. F G   C. X F   D. E F   E. X G   1.____

Explanation: The series consists of X's alternating with letters in alphabetical order. The next two letters would be F and X; therefore, A is the correct answer.

2. A B D C E F H
   A. G H   B. I G   C. G I   D. K L   E. I H   2.____

Explanation: If you compare this series with the alphabet, you will find that it goes along in pairs, the first pair in their usual order and the next pair in reverse order. The last letter given in the series is the second letter of the pair G-H, which is in reverse order. The first missing letter must, therefore, be G. The next pair of letters would be I-J, in that order; the second of the missing letters is I. The alternative you look for, then, is G I, which is lettered C.

DIRECTIONS: Each of the following questions presents a series of single letters. Five possible answers are given. From these choices, find what the next letter in the series should be if the series were to continue in this sequence. PRINT THE LETTER OF THE CORRECT ANSWER IN THE SPACE AT THE RIGHT.

1. B A C A D A E A F A G A
   A. H A   B. A H   C. K A   D. L A   E. A K   1.____

2. A B D C B D D B D E B D F B D G B
   A. H D   B. B G   C. D B   D. D H   E. D J   2.____

3. J I H G F E D C
   A. BC   B. CB   C. BA   D. A B   E. DC   3.____

4. Z Y X W V U T S R
   A. P Q   B. P O   C. O P   D. N P   E. Q P   4.____

5. X W V X U X T X S X R
   A. X O   B. Q X   C. X P   D. P X   E. X Q   5.____

6. K L N M O P R Q S T
   A. V U   B. U V   C. W V   D. V W   E. W U   6.____

7. A B C F E D G H I L K J M
   A. O N   B. N O   C. O M   D. M O   E. M N   7.____

2 (#5)

8. Z Y W X V U S T R Q O P N M
    A. K J   B. J K   C. K L   D. L K   E. L M

8.____

9. Y Z X W U V T S Q R P O M N
    A. K J   B. L K   C. K L   D. J K   E. M L

9.____

10. Z Y X U V W T S R O P Q N M L
    A. I K   B. K I   C. I J   D. K J   E. J I

10.____

11. A C E G I K M O Q
    A. S U   B. S T   C. R S   D. R T   E. U S

11.____

12. Z U X V T R P N L
    A. K L   B. K J   C. H J   D. L K   E. J H

12.____

13. Z W T Q N K H
    A. E B   B. E C   D. F B   D. F C   E. C F

13.____

14. A D G J M P S
    A. V W   B. U W   C. U V   D. V Y   E. W U

14.____

15. A D F I K N P S
    A. W U   B. U W   C. U X   D. U V   E. V U

15.____

KEY (CORRECT ANSWERS)

1. A	6. A	11. A
2. D	7. B	12. E
3. C	8. C	13. A
4. E	9. B	14. D
5. E	10. E	15. C

TEST 6

DIRECTIONS: Each of the following questions presents a series of single letters. Five possible answers are given. From these choices, you are to find what the next letter in the series should be if the series were to be continued in this sequence. *PRINT THE LETTER OF THE CORRECT ANSWER IN THE SPACE AT THE RIGHT.*

1. A C E D G I H K M L
   A. O P B. O Q C. Q P D. P Q E. Q O

2. Z X V W T R S P N O
   A. J K B. K J C. L K D. K L E. K I

3. B A D C F E H G J I L
   A. K N B. K M C. N K D. L K E. K L

4. Y Z W X U V S T Q R O P M
   A. L K B. K L C. N L D. N K E. L N

5. A B D C E F H G I J L K M N
   A. R P B. P O C. O P D. P Q E. Q P

6. A B C D F E G H I J L K M
   A. O N B. N O C. P O D. O P E. M N

7. Z Y X U V W T S R
   A. O P B. P O C. O N D. N O E. P Q

8. A B C B C D C D E D E F E
   A. G H B. G F C. E F D. F G E. F E

9. X V T R P F H J
   A. K L B. L M C. K M D. M N E. L N

10. C C F F I I L L V V S S P P M M
    A. K K B. I I C. J J D. H H E. G G

11. A N C O E P G
    A. H I B. R H C. R I D. Q I E. I Q

12. B D F H J L N
    A. P Q B. S Q C. R P D. P R E. Q S

13. Z X V T R P N
    A. J L B. M L C. L K D. M K E. L J

14. A B D G K
    A. L O B. O Q C. Q O D. P L E. P W

1. ____
2. ____
3. ____
4. ____
5. ____
6. ____
7. ____
8. ____
9. ____
10. ____
11. ____
12. ____
13. ____
14. ____

15. F H K O T R O   15.____
     A. J G   B. L F   C. K G   D. J F   E. K F

KEY (CORRECT ANSWERS)

1.	B	6.	B	11.	D
2.	E	7.	A	12.	D
3.	A	8.	D	13.	E
4.	D	9.	E	14.	E
5.	B	10.	C	15.	E

TEST 7

DIRECTIONS: Each of the following questions presents a series of single letters. Five possible answers are given. From these choices, you are to find what the next letter in the series should be if the series were to be continued in this sequence. *PRINT THE LETTER OF THE CORRECT ANSWER IN THE SPACE AT THE RIGHT.*

1. B B G G L L O O R R S S
   A. U U B. V V C. T T D. W W E. X X
   1.____

2. A C B D C E D F E G
   A. F G B. G H C. H F D. F H E. G F
   2.____

3. D H F J H L J N
   A. M N B. L N C. L O D. L P E. P N
   3.____

4. A C E F H J K M O
   A. M O Q B. R T P C. N Q O D. P T R E. P R T
   4.____

5. B G L Q V E J O
   A. P U B. T Y C. R W D. S X E. Y Z
   5.____

6. A F G B G H C H I D
   A. F K B. G L C. H M D. I N E. I J
   6.____

7. A K B L C M D N
   A. E M B. F N C. J L D. E J E. E O
   7.____

8. P R K M F H
   A. C E B. A C C. D F D. B D E. C E
   8.____

9. A G M S Y B H N
   A. P V B. Q W C. R X D. S Y E. T Z
   9.____

10. B E C F D G Y V X U
    A. W T B. W V C. V U D. T S E. U T
    10.____

KEY (CORRECT ANSWERS)

1. C 6. E
2. D 7. E
3. D 8. B
4. E 9. E
5. B 10. A

INTERVIEWING
EXAMINATION SECTION
TEST 1

DIRECTIONS: Each question or incomplete statement is followed by several suggested answers or completions. Select the one that BEST answers the question or completes the statement. *PRINT THE LETTER OF THE CORRECT ANSWER IN THE SPACE AT THE RIGHT.*

1. Of the methods given below for obtaining desired information from applicants, the one considered the BEST interviewing method is to
   A. work from an outline, asking the questions in the order in which they appear and requiring the applicant to give specific answers
   B. let the applicant tell what he has to say in his own way first, the interviewer then taking responsibility for asking questions on points not covered
   C. tell the applicant all the facts that it is necessary to have, then letting him give the information in any way he chooses
   D. verify all such facts as birth date, income, and past employment before seeing the applicant, then asking the applicant to fill in the remaining gaps when he is interviewed

1.____

2. Suppose an applicant objects to answering a question regarding his recent employment and asks, "What business is it of yours, young man?"
   In conducting the interview, the MOST constructive course of action for you to take under the circumstances would be to
   A. tell the applicant you have no intention of prying into his personal affairs and go on to the next question
   B. refer the applicant to your supervisor
   C. rephrase the question so that only a "Yes" or "No" answer is required
   D. explain why the question is being asked

2.____

3. An interview is BEST conducted in private PRIMARILY because
   A. the person interviewed will tend to be less self-conscious
   B. the interviewer will be able to maintain his continuity of thought better
   C. it will insure that the interview is "off the record"
   D. people tend to "show off" before an audience

3.____

4. An interviewer will be better able to understand the person interviewed and his problems if he recognizes that much of the person's behavior is due to motives
   A. which are deliberate
   B. of which he is unaware
   C. which are inexplicable
   D. which are kept under control

4.____

5. When an applicant is repeatedly told that "everything will be all right," the effect that can USUALLY be expected is that he will
    A. develop overt negativistic reactions toward the agency
    B. become too closely identified with the interviewer
    C. doubt the interviewer's ability to understand and help with his problems
    D. have greater confidence in the interviewer

6. While interviewing a client, it is PREFERABLE that the interviewer
    A. take no notes in order to avoid disturbing the client
    B. focus primary attention on the client while the client is talking
    C. take no notes in order to impress upon the client the interviewer's ability to remember all the pertinent facts of his case
    D. record all the details in order to show the client that what he says is important

7. During an interview, a curious applicant asks several questions about the interviewer's private life.
   As the interviewer, you should
    A. refuse to answer such questions
    B. answer his questions fully
    C. explain that your primary concern is with his problems and that discussion of your personal affairs will not be helpful in meeting his needs
    D. explain that it is the responsibility of the interviewer to ask questions and not to answer them

8. An interviewer can BEST establish a good relationship with the person being interviewed by
    A. assuming casual interest in the statements made by the person being interviewed
    B. asking questions which enable the person to show pride in his knowledge
    C. taking the point of view of the person interviewed
    D. showing a genuine interest in the person

9. An interviewer's attention must be directed toward himself as well as toward the person interviewed.
   This statement means that the interviewer should
    A. keep in mind the extent to which his own prejudices may influence his judgment
    B. rationalize the statements made by the person interviewed
    C. gain the respect and confidence of the person interviewed
    D. avoid being too impersonal

10. More complete expression will be obtained from a person being interviewed if the interviewer can create the impression that
    A. the data secured will become part of a permanent record
    B. official information must be accurate in every detail
    C. it is the duty of the person interviewed to give accurate data
    D. the person interviewed is participating in a discussion of his own problems

11. The practice of asking leading questions should be avoided in an interview because the
    A. interviewer risks revealing his attitudes to the person being interviewed
    B. interviewer may be led to ignore the objective attitudes of the person interviewed
    C. answers may be unwarrantedly influenced
    D. person interviewed will resent the attempt to lead him and will be less cooperative

12. A good technique for the interviewer to use in an effort to secure reliable data and to reduce the possibility of misunderstanding is to
    A. use casual undirected conversation, enabling the person being interviewed to talk about himself, and thus secure the desired information
    B. adopt the procedure of using direct questions regularly
    C. extract the desired information from the person being interviewed by putting him on the defensive
    D. explain to the person being interviewed the information desired and the reason for needing it

13. In interviewing an applicant, your attitude toward his veracity should be that the information he has furnished you is
    A. *untruthful* until you have had an opportunity to check the information
    B. *truthful* only insofar as verifiable facts are concerned
    C. *untruthful* because clients tend to interpret everything in their own favor
    D. *truthful* until you have information to the contrary

14. When an agency assigns its most experienced interviewers to conduct initial interviews with applicants, the MOST important reason for its action is that
    A. experienced workers are always older and, therefore, command the respect of applicants
    B. the applicant may be given a complete understanding of the procedures to be followed and the time involved in obtaining assistance
    C. applicants with fraudulent intentions will be detected, and prevented from obtaining further services from the agency
    D. the applicant may be given an understanding of the purpose of the assistance program and of the bases for granting assistance, in addition to the routine information

15. In conducting the first interview with an applicant, you should
    A. ask questions requiring "Yes" or "No" answers in order to simplify the interview
    B. rephrase several of the key questions as a check on his previous statements
    C. let him tell his own story while keeping him to the relevant facts
    D. avoid showing any sympathy for the applicant while he is revealing his personal needs and problems

16. When an interview opens an interview by asking the client direct questions about his work, it is very likely that the client will feel
    A. that the interview is interested in him
    B. at ease if his work has been good
    C. free to discuss his attitudes toward his work
    D. that good reports are of great importance to the interviewer in his thinking

17. When an interviewer does NOT understand the meaning of a response that a client has made, the interviewer should
    A. proceed to another topic
    B. state that he does not understand and ask for clarification
    C. act as if he understands so that the client's confidence in him should not be shaken
    D. ask the client to rephrase his response

18. When an interviewer makes a response which brings on a high degree of resistance in the client, he should
    A. apologize and rephrase his remark in a less evocative manner
    B. accept the resistance on the part of the client
    C. ignore the client's resistance
    D. recognize that little more will be accomplished in the interview and suggest another appointment

19. Most definitions of interviewing would NOT include the following as a necessary aspect:
    A. The interviewer and client meet face-to-face and talk things out
    B. The client is experiencing considerable emotional disturbance
    C. A valuable learning opportunity is provided for the client
    D. The interviewer brings a special competence to the relationship

20. A powerful dynamic in the interviewing process and often the very *antonym* of its counterpart in the instructional process is
    A. encouraging accuracy
    B. emphasizing structure
    C. pointing up sequential and orderly thinking
    D. processing ambiguity and equivocation

21. Interviewing techniques are frequently useful in working with clients. A basic fundamental is an atmosphere which may BEST be described as
    A. non-threatening
    B. motivating for creativity
    C. highly charged to stimulate excitement
    D. fairly-well structured

22. In interviewing the disadvantaged client, the subtle technique of steering away from high-level educational and vocational plans must be *replaced* by
    A. a wait-and-see explanation to the client
    B. the use of prediction tables to determine possibilities and probabilities of overcoming this condition

C. avoidance in discussing controversial issues of deprivation
D. encouragement and concrete consideration for planning his future

23. The process of collecting, analyzing, synthesizing, and interpreting information about the client should be
    A. completed prior to interviewing
    B. completed early in the interviewing process
    C. limited to a type of interviewing which is primarily diagnostic in purpose
    D. continuously pursued throughout interviewing

23.____

24. Catharsis, the "emotional unloading" of the client's feelings, has a value in the early stages of interviewing because it accomplishes all BUT which one of the following goals?
    It
    A. relieves strong physiological tensions in the client
    B. increases the client's anxiety and aggrandizes his motivation to continue counseling
    C. provides a strong substitute for "acting out" the client's feelings
    D. releases emotional energy which the client has been using to bulwark his defenses

24.____

25. In the interviewing process, the interviewer should *usually* give information
    A. whenever it is needed
    B. at the end of the process
    C. in the introductory interview
    D. just before the client would ordinarily request it

25.____

KEY (CORRECT ANSWERS)

1.	B		11.	C
2.	D		12.	D
3.	A		13.	D
4.	B		14.	D
5.	C		15.	C
6.	B		16.	D
7.	C		17.	B
8.	D		18.	B
9.	A		19.	B
10.	D		20.	D

21. A
22. D
23. D
24. B
25. A

TEST 2

DIRECTIONS: Each question or incomplete statement is followed by several suggested answers or completions. Select the one that BEST answers the question or completes the statement. *PRINT THE LETTER OF THE CORRECT ANSWER IN THE SPACE AT THE RIGHT.*

1. Of the following problems that might affect the conduct and outcome of an interview, the MOST troublesome and usually the MOST difficult for the interviewer to control is the
    A. tendency of the interviewee to anticipate the needs and preferences of the interviewer
    B. impulse to cut the interviewee off when he seems to have reached the end of an idea
    C. tendency of interviewee attitude to bias the results
    D. tendency of the interviewer to do most of the talking

   1.____

2. The supervisor MOST likely to be a good interviewer is one who
    A. is adept at manipulating people and circumstances toward his objective
    B. is able to put himself in the position of the interviewee
    C. gets the more difficult questions out of the way at the beginning of the interview
    D. develops one style and technique that can be used in any type of interview

   2.____

3. A good interviewer guards against the tendency to form an overall opinion about an interviewee on the basis of a single aspect of the interviewee's makeup.
   This statement refers to a well-known source of error in interviewing known as the
    A. assumption error   B. expectancy error
    C. extension effect   D. halo effect

   3.____

4. In conducting an "exit interview" with an employee who is leaving voluntarily, the interview's MAIN objective should be to
    A. see that the employee leaves with a good opinion of the organization
    B. learn the true reasons for the employee's resignation
    C. find out if the employee would consider a transfer
    D. try to get the employee to remain on the job

   4.____

5. During an interview, an interviewee unexpectedly discloses a relevant but embarrassing personal fact.
   It would be BEST for the interviewer to
    A. listen calmly, avoiding any gesture or facial expression that would suggest approval or disapproval of what is related
    B. change the subject, since further discussion in this area may reveal other embarrassing, but irrelevant, personal facts

   5.____

C. apologize to the interviewee for having led him to reveal such a fact and promise not to do so again
D. bring the interview to a close as quickly as possible in order to avoid a discussion which may be distressing to the interviewee

6. Suppose that, while you are interviewing an applicant for a position in your office, you notice a contradiction in facts in two of his responses.
For you to call the contradictions to his attention would be
    A. *inadvisable*, because it reduces the interviewee's level of participation
    B. *advisable*, because getting the facts is essential to a successful interview
    C. *inadvisable*, because the interviewer should use more subtle techniques to resolve any discrepancies
    D. *advisable*, because the interviewee should be impressed with the necessity for giving consistent answers

7. An interviewer should be aware that an undesirable result of including "leading questions" in an interview is to
    A. cause the interviewee to give a "yes" or "no" answers with qualification or explanation
    B. encourage the interviewee to discuss irrelevant topics
    C. encourage the interviewee to give more meaningful information
    D. reduce the validity of the information obtained from the interviewee

8. The kind of interview which is particularly helpful in getting an employee to tell about his complaints and grievances is one in which
    A. a pattern has been worked out involving a sequence of exact questions to be asked
    B. the interviewee is expected to support his statements with specific evidence
    C. the interviewee is not made to answer specific questions but is encouraged to talk freely
    D. the interviewer has specific items on which he wishes to get or give information

9. Suppose you are scheduled to interview an employee under your supervision concerning a health problem. You know that some of the questions you will be asking him will seem embarrassing to him, and that he may resist answering these questions.
In general, to hold these questions for the last part of the interview would be
    A. *desirable*; the intervening time period gives the interviewer an opportunity to plan how to ask these sensitive questions.
    B. *undesirable*; the employee will probably feel that he has been tricked when he suddenly must answer embarrassing questions
    C. *desirable*; the employee will probably have increased confidence in the interviewer and be more willing to answer these questions
    D. *undesirable*; questions that are important should not be deferred until the end of the interview

10. In conducting an interview, the BEST types of questions with which to begin the interview are those which the person interviewed is
    A. willing and able to answer
    B. willing but unable to answer
    C. able but unwilling to answer
    D. unable and unwilling to answer

11. In order to determine accurately a child's age, it is BEST for an interviewer to rely on
    A. the child's grade in school
    B. what the mother says
    C. birth records
    D. a library card

12. In his first interview with a new employee, it would be LEAST appropriate for a unit supervisor to
    A. find out the employee's preference for the several types of jobs to which he is able to assign him
    B. determine whether the employee will make good promotion material
    C. inform the employee of what his basic job responsibilities will be
    D. inquire about the employee's education and previous employment

13. If an interviewer takes care to phrase his questions carefully and precisely, the result will MOST probably be that
    A. he will be able to determine whether the person interviewed is being truthful
    B. the free flow of the interview will be lost
    C. he will get the information he wants
    D. he will ask stereotyped questions and narrow the scope of the interview

14. When, during an interview, is the person interviewed LEAST likely to be cautious about what he tells the interviewer?
    A. Shortly after the beginning when the questions normally suggest pleasant associations to the person interviewed
    B. As long as the interviewer keeps his questions to the point
    C. At the point where the person interviewed gains a clear insight into the area being discussed
    D. When the interview appears formally ended and goodbyes are being said

15. In an interview held for the purpose of getting information from the person interviewed, it is sometimes desirable for the interviewer to repeat the answer he has received to a question.
    For the interviewer to rephrase such an answer in his own words is good practice MAINLY because it
    A. gives the interviewer time to make up his next question
    B. gives the person interviewed a chance to correct any possible misunderstanding
    C. gives the person interviewed the feeling that the interviewer considers his answer important
    D. prevents the person interviewed from changing his answer

16. There are several methods of formulating questions during an interview. The particular method used should be adapted to the interview problems presented by the person being questioned.
    Of the following methods of formulating questions during an interview, the ACCEPTABLE one is for the interviewer to ask questions which
    A. incorporate several items in order to allow a cooperative interviewee freedom to organize his statements
    B. are ambiguous in order to foil a distrustful interviewee
    C. suggest the correct answer in order to assist an interviewee who appears confused
    D. would help an otherwise unresponsive interviewee to become more responsive

    16.____

17. For an interviewer to permit the person being interviewed to read the data the interviewer writes as he records the person's responses on a routine departmental form is
    A. *desirable*, because it serves to assure the person interviewed that his responses are being recorded accurately
    B. *undesirable*, because it prevents the interviewer from clarifying uncertain points by asking additional questions
    C. *desirable*, because it makes the time that the person interviewed must wait while the answer is written seem shorter
    D. *undesirable*, because it destroys the confidentiality of the interview

    17.____

18. Of the following methods of conducting an interview, the BEST is to
    A. ask questions with "yes" or "no" answers
    B. listen carefully and ask only questions that are pertinent
    C. fire questions at the interviewee so that he must answer sincerely and briefly
    D. read standardized questions to the person being interviewed

    18.____

KEY (CORRECT ANSWERS)

1.	A	11.	C
2.	B	12.	B
3.	D	13.	C
4.	B	14.	D
5.	A	15.	B
6.	B	16.	D
7.	D	17.	A
8.	C	18.	B
9.	C		
10.	A		

www.ingramcontent.com/pod-product-compliance
Lightning Source LLC
Chambersburg PA
CBHW082207300426
44117CB00016B/2703